PREGNANCY: OLDER WOMEN

An Essential Guide

Need — 2 — Know

Jo Johnson

First published in Great Britain in 2009 by
Need2Know
Remus House
Coltsfoot Drive
Peterborough
PE2 9JX
Telephone 01733 898103
Fax 01733 313524
www.need2knowbooks.co.uk

Need2Know is an imprint of Forward Press Ltd.
www.forwardpress.co.uk
All Rights Reserved
© Jo Johnson 2009
SB ISBN 978-1-86144-074-7
Cover photograph: Jupiter Images

Contents

Introduction

Increasing numbers of couples are delaying starting a family until later in life; in fact some figures suggest that there is a steeper incline in the amount of women having children after the age of 30 than those in the preceding years. The reasons why this occurs are varied and range from couples wishing to gain greater financial stability before a baby is considered, to the amount of women wanting to pursue and succeed in a career. There are also the less controlled issues such as difficulties in conceiving to finding a suitable partner to start a family with.

There are many advantages of waiting to have a family until you are ready such as being prepared emotionally and financially, feeling as though you have all you want in your personal life and maybe your domestic arrangements too.

All of these are very good reasons, but there are also women, even those in their teens or 20s, who may struggle to conceive naturally if at all, and this is something that many people may have to discover and cope with in the future. For these people, there are more options available than ever before and fertility treatments seem to be on the increase.

A healthy and pro-active attitude to fertility and conception can be a very good start for many couples and it may be helpful to understand that some things take time and patience. Having a positive mental attitude and good physical health can play a great role in how you deal with your situation.

Disclaimer

This book is for general information about pregnancy. It is not intended to replace professional medical advice. It can be used alongside medical advice, but anyone with concerns about their pregnancy is strongly advised to consult their healthcare professional.

Chapter One

Older Mothers and Pregnancy

Having a baby is something that most of us take very seriously and we want to provide the best possible lifestyle for the whole family. Often this is why some women decide to wait until they are slightly older and more secure before they try to conceive. There are, however, some issues that may need some consideration as occasionally it is not all plain sailing. For example, even though we might all be aware of the stigmas attached to very young mothers (rightly or wrongly), some older parents may also find they are the subject of public scrutiny and opinion.

There are also issues concerning expectations when the baby is born; some women may have waited until they feel more psychologically ready and then go on to find they do not cope as well as they expected. Whatever the reason for having a family later on, there are numerous issues that may arise and it is often helpful to address some of them or even simply raise your own awareness of the possible difficulties that you may face regarding conception and raising a child.

What defines the term 'older mother'?

The expression 'older mother' may sound like a phrase taken from the front page of a tabloid newspaper, but it is in fact a legitimately used term used to identify those of a certain age and was produced for perfectly sound reasons.

Where did the term 'older mother' come from?

The term has developed in usage since the publication of national statistics in 2007 that showed a clear trend in the rise of women opting to start a family in the latter years of their fertility, particularly in the over-35 category. It is around this time that a female's level of fertility starts to decline quite rapidly, making the chances of a natural conception increasingly less likely as time progresses. This also coincides with an increase in possible complications throughout the pregnancy and birth and a rise in the incidence of birth defects.

Another contributing factor to the growing trend of older parents is the development and availability of fertility treatments and assistance. The use of IVF (in vitro fertilisation) and other assisted conception methods has allowed people the chance to try for a baby later on who may previously have been unable to.

It is not just the female parent who seems to be getting older as men too are also choosing to have a family later on, with a rise in the number of over 30s occurring alongside a decrease in those in their 20s.

What if I don't like being called an 'older mother'?

Some women may find that they really do not like to be labelled with this title (often those in their 30s feel and look younger), others because they don't like labels in general. If you really find it offensive, you are quite entitled to ask people not to put you under this umbrella. However, healthcare professionals such as your midwife and GP will need to identify that you are over 35 in your notes and any correspondence to other professionals as there are some very serious risks involved with those pregnant over the age of 35 and this needs to be identified. You may find that your age will require some such defining term to be used because of this.

Other terms that may be used

It is not just the term 'older mother' that may be used to identify those over the age of 35, and due to the nature of the alternatives many women actually prefer for this title to be used.

In some places, it is not uncommon for the phrase 'elderly primagravida' to be used, which a lot of women find offensive as at the age of 35 using the word 'elderly' is seen as somewhat inappropriate. However, some form of identification needs to be used.

Society and stigmas

Modern society in which we live seems to be full of people's opinions, attitudes and stigmas often given with no plausible reason, which serve to do nothing except affect people negatively. There are endless situations that cause the public to pass judgement or comment, even on subjects that years ago would have caused little effect on anyone. In previous generations for example, how many families had more than five or 10 children? The answer is plenty of them, so realistically it would have meant that the mother could still be having pregnancies into her late 30s or 40s. This was not seen as abnormal or unusual at all, whereas today some people could find this extraordinary and comment not just on the number of children, but on the mother's age too.

Fortunately, however, these attitudes are not based on anything other than misconception. Statistics prove that there are more women waiting until their 30s and beyond to have children than in previous years so the only unusual thing about it is that often this is the first child they are having rather than one of many offspring.

Negative stigmas

Negative stigmas and attitudes tend to have arisen due to increased use of fertility treatments and people often discuss the expression 'just because you can doesn't mean you should'. In other words, just because the technology exists to impregnate an older woman, doesn't mean that it is 'right' to do so. Many people argue that nature provides women with the menopause as a way of protecting society, meaning that a younger mother will be able to care for her children during their dependent years. They worry that an older mother may not be around to see their family grow up and that technology has merely made childbirth and child rearing more problematic. However, It could be

'Statistics prove that there are more women waiting until their 30s and beyond to have children than in previous years, so the only unusual thing about it is that often this is the first child they are having rather than one of many offspring.'

mentioned, that disease, accidents and social issues can also leave younger mothers unable to raise their children similarly, so this argument does not particularly stand up well to criticism.

Due to these issues (and many others), there are guidelines in the UK that exist to ensure those who are older and seeking help with fertility are healthy enough to carry a child, that they understand they may face certain sociological barriers and that they understand the entire fertility process and how it affects them physically, socially, mentally and emotionally.

Positive attitudes

Despite all the negative attitudes that may or may not arise because of a person's age, there are many people who have very positive attitudes towards older parents in general.

For example, plenty of people feel that older parents are in a far better position to care for their children as they are less interested in maintaining a hectic social life and are ready to exchange nights out for stories at bedtime. Also more likely is the parent's ability to provide financial security without having to rely on financial assistance in the form of benefits (although do remember that you are entitled to some payments and these shouldn't be overlooked).

People may also feel that those who have waited for a child have planned the event and will therefore care for the child as it is wanted. This does not suggest that those who don't plan a child do not care for the baby, but is simply an observation of public opinion.

Whatever your scenario, you will no doubt come across both negative and positive attitudes about parenting and pregnancy in general and it is important to remember that you are an individual and no one will encounter your experiences in the same way; your life is unique.

Support from others

Even those in their early 20s will feel the benefit of support from those around them and you are no different. Now is the time to pull on your friends and family for support, don't be afraid to ask them if you need it.

If you do receive negativity from the public or even people you know, just remember why you have waited this long to begin with and focus on all the positives that having a child will bring.

As you will find out in later chapters, older mums are frequently told of the increased risks of being over 35 and pregnant and the amount of negative information you are exposed to can be concerning. While these risks are real and are something you may have to face, the majority of pregnancies even in the 'older mothers' category are problem free and enjoyed by the prospective parents. It is normally during these times that you may feel the need to lean on others for support.

What will people think?

The general attitude of the public seems to be fairly supportive of older mums until their early 40s. You may find that there seem to be a few people who have negative opinions of older mothers perhaps because they believe that nature should be permitted to take its own course, or maybe they think that women have delayed motherhood for their own reasons and may have sought medical assistance to get pregnant. Try not to focus on these perceptions, as your pregnancy is very special and nothing should spoil or mar this wonderful time for you. Being pregnant at any age is a blessing and something that should always be treasured.

At times, most parents have to face adversity for the sake of their children and often a thick skin is needed to cope, so letting people negatively affect you now will only serve to upset you and affect the pregnancy.

What about older fathers?

Older fathers seem to escape the public criticism more easily than women, possibly because they do not have the same biological clock, and perhaps because, in general, people see the child rearing process as a predominantly female job.

It may be possible to hear an infrequent comment about a new father's age but somewhat unfairly, it does seem to be women who take the most criticism.

What to expect and how to deal with it

The reality of pregnancy is the same for everyone regardless of age; you are likely to experience a rollercoaster of emotions during the pregnancy, face many worries and anxieties about giving birth or raising a child and also how you will cope in the long term.

Mums who have waited until later for children tend to agree they make very good parents as they are more patient, have a better understanding of parenting, are more financially capable of providing for their children and on the whole are more organised as they planned for parenthood, often for many years. This does not mean that they do not feel the pressures of pregnancy and family life, just that they may be more equipped to deal with them if they do crop up.

Expectations of conception

Perhaps you have spent the last few years building a stable base, enjoying your free time, working towards your goals and now you feel ready to start the family you always dreamed of; this is great news. Unfortunately, there are a few women who may find that they have been so busy laying down these foundations they have neglected to pay attention to their fertility.

As already mentioned, your chances of a natural conception are lessened quite significantly after the age of 35 and although this is perhaps nature's way it is something that can cause problems.

If you have timed everything perfectly, know your menstrual cycle and your body well, it can still take some length of time to conceive following which you may find that a little extra help is required. One such way is to understand and know exactly when you are ovulating. To do this you need to know how long your cycle is. Some women have a 21 day cycle, others will find they may have up to a 32 day cycle or even longer; this is fine if it is normal for you.

To find out when you are ovulating, you need to work out when your period is next due and count 14 days backward to pinpoint exactly when you release an egg. You can try intercourse a day or two before this and up to the time of ovulation, as healthy sperm can live in the female body for many hours while they try to find a viable egg to fertilise.

If you have an irregular cycle and find it difficult to find an exact date of ovulation you could take a guess around the average time of your cycle or try using a home ovulation predictor kit, but please be aware that these may be costly.

Expectations of the pregnancy

So much has been written about pregnancy and what to expect that it seems we should all automatically know exactly what is going to happen, when and what it will feel like and so on, but in reality, nothing prepares you for the experience and each person will have their own story to tell. For instance, not all women have cravings while others have some very strange ones, some women find it exhausting, worrying how they will cope with a newborn when they are already so tired while others are full of energy and enthusiasm.

One minute you feel very excited about becoming a parent, the next you may be plunged into panic worrying if something will go wrong. Whatever age, most pregnant women feel like this from time to time and sometimes spending too long reading other people's stories can be detrimental to your experience as many printed accounts are of tragedy or troubles.

Expectations of the labour

It can be quite easy to find yourself spending more time worrying about the labour and delivery than you spend delighting in your pregnancy. Fear is a strong emotion and many women will admit to spending time worrying about something. Try not to become too anxious, women give birth every day and usually go on to have more children in the future knowing exactly what labour feels like. On occasion, women have reported they overestimated the pain they expected and that it wasn't quite what they were expecting at all.

'To find out when you are ovulating you need to work out when your period is next due and count 14 days backward to pinpoint exactly when you release an egg.'

It can be very helpful to discuss your fears with your midwife and as the pregnancy progresses you can discuss the different types of pain relief available to you and whether or not you would like to include them into your birth plan.

You will also find out that, for various reasons, being slightly older increases the risks and as a result more medical attention is needed during the pregnancy and labour but do remember that it is still very possible to have a totally natural birth just as you'd planned.

How old is too old?

On a personal level, you may feel that there is no way of putting an age to this question and plenty of people feel the same. To lots of women (and men) age is simply a number and doesn't bear any influence over the way you feel, how you live your life or what decisions and choices you make. There is really no right or wrong answer to this question as it is a matter of opinion. However, many fertility clinics do enforce age limits on their clients mainly to protect the woman from the possible risks to her own health that can arise from carrying a pregnancy.

This is indeed an evocative subject and has been a major part of public debate for many years and will most likely continue to be so. Unfortunately, due to Mother Nature, the argument seems to be directed largely at women while older fathers escape public scrutiny and criticism.

Deciding when it is the right time

Some people may argue that there is never a right time to start a family and it is not something that can be planned into your schedule. To a degree this may be true as your conception might not occur exactly when you planned it or perhaps your birth control failed and you have fallen pregnant by accident.

However, usually people who have waited to have a baby have always had a general idea of when they want to try for a baby and they know when the time feels right.

'It can be very helpful to discuss your fears with your midwife and as the pregnancy progresses you can discuss the different types of pain relief available to you and whether or not you would like to include them into your birth plan.'

Whether you planned the pregnancy or not, it seems like now is the right time for you and you are getting ready to share your life with a little one.

Is it possible to leave it too late?

The quick answer to this is yes. It may be that you have left it too late to conceive either independently or with treatment, though you may find the age limits for fertility assistance are higher than you think.

We have all read about the extremes of parental ages in the newspapers or heard about them on the news and we might have our own opinions of this. The Human Fertilisation and Embryology Authority (HEFA), who are the UK's governing body on issues of fertility treatments, do not stipulate age limits as such and it remains the discretion of the clinician offering treatment to decide.

Due to this, several health authorities enforce their own upper age limits and this may influence your decision as to which clinic you select. Do remember though, that high financial costs may arise if you are selective where you seek treatment.

Those who do not wish to seek help with fertility should be aware that it is possible to become pregnant during the menopause and the general consensus is that a woman must be period free for at least a year before she is considered to no longer be fertile.

Am I pregnant or is it the menopause?

Of course, not all older mothers plan their pregnancy and little surprises can catch out anyone, even those using a trusted form of contraception. In fact, plenty of women in their 40s and even 50s mistakenly believe their disrupted cycle, changing body and emotional changes are caused by the onset of the menopause only to find out later that they are pregnant.

It is not uncommon to discover the signs and symptoms of menopause and early pregnancy are very similar and though you used contraception, it might have failed.

Any changes to your cycle that are very different from your normal routine should be investigated and often your GP will want to do a pregnancy test in the first instance. It is important to understand that if you are taking the contraceptive pill and fall pregnant, you will still produce a regular withdrawal bleed every month. As this is not a true period, you should consider any disruptions and changes as possible pregnancies too.

The chance of becoming pregnant during the menopause is still a very real risk and many women around the world have found themselves with an unexpected pregnancy that they didn't think was possible. Therefore it is very important to be aware that you are still fertile during this time, albeit with a reduced level of fertility.

'The early stages of menopause and those commonly associated with pregnancy can be very difficult to distinguish and many women have been "caught out" mistaking one for the other.'

Similarities between pregnancy and menopausal symptoms

The early stages of menopause and those commonly associated with pregnancy can be very difficult to distinguish and many women have been 'caught out' mistaking one for the other. It is especially easy to confuse the two if you are over the age of 35 and have not had a particularly regular cycle throughout your life.

Commonly shared symptoms are sore breasts, mood swings, changes in appetite, feeling hot, tiredness, irritability and, of course, changes to your cycle.

Spotting can also happen both in early pregnancy and with early stages of menopause and if irregular for you, should be investigated.

Taking a pregnancy test

For a woman believing she is going through the menopause, it may seem ridiculous to take a pregnancy test and many women may feel a little embarrassed buying one, but it really is important.

Do not ignore the signs and symptoms, take a test when you can as the longer you leave it, the fewer the options available to you. You may even miss the time scale during which many important tests can be offered.

When to see your GP

Most importantly, if you believe you have been through the menopause and have experienced any bleeding, it is essential that this is investigated and you should make an appointment with your GP very soon.

If however, you have taken a pregnancy test and achieved a positive result, you really should book in with your GP as soon as you can as you will need to be monitored and offered tests to see if you or your baby is at risk of any complications.

Summing Up

When people refer to older mothers they generally mean those over the age of 35 as this is when levels of fertility start to decline quite steeply in comparison to previous years. The reasons for women waiting until their later years of fertility are wide and varied and can range from wanting to establish a career first, making themselves financially stable with solid financial arrangements, or simply because they enjoy not having any ties or have just not had the time.

Women in this category should be aware however, that due to the decline in fertility it may take longer than they had previously anticipated to conceive, and that there are more risks associated with being pregnant as an older woman than as a younger woman.

With this in mind though, women should not be afraid of starting a family as many women go on to have very healthy pregnancies and children well into their 40s.

Chapter Two

How Age Affects Fertility

Many women over the age of 35 do not suffer any complications at all. Unfortunately though, not all will conceive without problems, carry a healthy pregnancy to term or give birth to a healthy 'normal' baby. This shows the importance of older women understanding any potential risks involved in the conception and birthing process in order to make an informed decision regarding their family planning.

Most people are familiar with the expression concerning 'the biological clock ticking' and generally understand that as we get older and approach menopausal age, our fertility decreases until eventually we are no longer able to become pregnant naturally.

Experts tend to agree that a woman is at her most fertile between the ages of 20 and 24 years, although the chance of a pregnancy exists from the first ovulation to the year after menopause has ended.

This does not mean that women may struggle to conceive at the age of 25, but there is a very small decrease in the level of your fertility. This decrease in fertility continues on a gradual decline to the age of 35 when the chances fall more steeply, and it is predicted that you will be half as fertile as you were at 25 years of age. The chances continue to lessen at quite a sharp rate past the age of 35.

Age plays a large role in a person's ability to conceive a healthy pregnancy, and although the effects are not as obvious, men may not escape from the consequences of age either.

The effects of age on eggs

As we age, the chances of conceiving are lessened for many reasons as nature dictates. When we are young, we have a huge reserve of eggs in our ovaries, in fact we are born with the most plentiful supply we will ever have. Along with this, younger women usually tend to have more regular menstrual cycles and ovulation (once adolescence has ended) and a healthy balance of hormones which allow the eggs to mature and be released when they should.

The aging process can affect eggs in many ways. Firstly, along with the amount of eggs in the ovaries decreasing, so too does the quality of the eggs. Secondly, our hormonal balance becomes less finely tuned and our cycles can become less regular with an increase in possible gynaecological problems. Finally, the cervix and the mucous that surrounds it undergo changes that may affect a woman's ability to conceive naturally or carry a healthy pregnancy to term.

It is important to mention that there is also a slightly higher risk of miscarriage in those over the age of 35. It is believed that this relates to the womb's ability to manage a developing foetus (though many pregnancies in those of a younger age also result in a miscarriage).

'The number of sperm produced by a healthy male does not seem to decrease with age like the female supply of eggs.'

The effects of age on sperm

Unlike the female body, the male does not have a useable supply of sperm from birth; they do make up for this by creating an abundant supply during puberty making several million often very potent and healthy sperm every day. The number of sperm produced by a healthy male does not seem to decrease with age like the female supply of eggs.

Despite this, there are arguments to suggest that the quality of a man's sperm may decrease over time, though whether lifestyle is the major contributing factor is open for debate as alcohol and tobacco consumption may greatly affect the sperm in many cases.

There is also significant evidence that shows mutations of sperm can occur as men age, also because of the huge number of sperm that are produced every day. Each new 'batch' that is made is a replica of the last one; this process occurs several times a day so it is reasonable to assume that sometimes an exact replica cannot be achieved and thus the chances of an abnormality may be slightly greater.

The effects of age and the ability to carry a healthy pregnancy

Type in the term 'older mother' into a search engine and many women will be daunted by the results produced. While there may be some elements of truth to the information such as a higher incidence of miscarriage or foetal developmental problems, the amount of women over the age of 35 who carry a healthy pregnancy and give birth to a bouncing baby is still very high.

Diabetes and high blood pressure

It is true that there are increased risks in developing diabetes, having high blood pressure or enduring problems with the placenta that are more commonly associated with older mothers. These issues can also affect younger mums-to-be and may be somewhat avoided by having a healthy lifestyle and a good level of general fitness and health before conception occurs. To some extent, women may have more control than they think concerning these areas and can alter their lifestyle before they try to fall pregnant.

In any case, modern antenatal and delivery units are now very well equipped to monitor and manage patients who carry an increased risk of these problems.

The greatest worry for older women and couples is the risk of having a child with some form of genetic defect. Unfortunately, there is a significant increased risk of this happening in those over the age of 35, and an even greater risk in those over the age of 40.

Your GP will be able to explain these risks further and also describe the kinds of tests that may be carried out to detect the likelihood of this happening and explain the choices you have open to you if an abnormality is detected.

The last risk of leaving it until later to get pregnant is the increased risk of miscarriage which is discussed later on.

Increased gynaecological problems

Although the largest contributory factor of decreased fertility in older women is the quality of eggs released, there are some gynaecological conditions that may inhibit a healthy conception and pregnancy.

Endometriosis

This condition occurs when the cells from the inside of the womb migrate to the other pelvic organs and abdominal tissues causing increased pain and bleeding.

The condition typically appears in those in their 20s and 30s and can often be easily overcome. However, if it is not treated, it can lead to further complications which are more difficult to treat and can affect your chances of conception.

Fibroids

Another complication that can inhibit fertility is the likelihood of developing fibroids. These are benign tumours of the womb that can grow on either the outer surface or actually inside the womb. Some women may develop a single fibroid, while others may develop multiple growths. The incidence of fibroids does tend to increase with age and, as they can grow slowly, often don't present any problems until they are fairly sizeable.

In most cases, fibroids can be treated leaving no long term effects, but in a few cases a hysterectomy may be the only option. For those who do not know they have a fibroid and go on to conceive, the risk of a miscarriage is greater, the way in which the embryo attaches to the wall of the womb can be affected and the way in which a developing foetus grows may be affected.

Problematic periods

Another factor may be troublesome periods and heavy blood loss over the years. This occurrence can cause women to develop a negative attitude towards fertility when in fact for a lot of these women, pregnancy and giving birth can actually relieve some of these problems.

Assistance for women hoping to conceive

Fortunately, medical science and research has found many solutions to help women who are concerned that their age may be affecting their fertility.

There are now more choices and options available to women and couples than before, and these are a lot more accessible than they once were. It is, however, important to act on any concerns as soon as they are raised as this will optimise your chances of becoming pregnant with minimal invasive procedure.

Understand your cycle

There are many things a woman can do to assist her chances of becoming pregnant.

First of all, it is important to understand your own cycle and know when you are most likely to conceive. Using an ovulation predictor kit can be very helpful in determining this. Making significant lifestyle changes to reduce stress or excess body weight, or cutting down on alcohol or smoking, can be very positive steps in improving your chances of conceiving a pregnancy or indeed being a suitable candidate for fertility treatment in the future.

Most experts agree that if you are a woman over the age of 35, and have been trying for a baby for at least a year, it is reasonable to make an appointment with your GP to ask what your next steps should be. For everyone else, it is recommended that waiting until you have been having regular and unprotected sex for at least two years before considering asking for fertility assistance.

It is important to understand that the longer you leave it to seek help, the fewer your chances of successful conception are. It is equally important to understand that instant results are not always likely and to some degree a

'Fortunately medical science and research has found many solutions to help women who are concerned that their age may be affecting their fertility.'

large amount of patience is necessary. Some experts and professionals also feel that there may be an unreasonable and disproportionate expectation from couples regarding fertility and this may be something that needs addressing in the future. In other words, couples should not delay childbirth and simply assume that some fertility treatments can be relied upon for a successful conception as this is unrealistic and the chances of success are in fact still quite low.

Your partner's fertility

It is also important to recognise that men too can suffer from problems with their fertility. Tests may show that you are still fertile and it is actually your partner who is less fertile; occasionally these problems can also be overcome.

Also a significant consideration is the financial implication of pursuing fertility treatment. While most people feel that a price probably shouldn't be put on wanting or raising a child, there may be financial implications, sometimes so significant that the decision to proceed could be out of your hands.

Fertility treatment is not for everyone and careful consideration should be given before commencing any programme of treatment. In fact, it can be very useful to contact others who have already travelled this route to find out exactly what it entails on a more personal level, or ask your GP or nurse if there is a counselling service available for prospective fertility patients.

Summing Up

Women over the age of 35 are more at risk of having difficulty conceiving as the quality of the female egg starts to decrease from this time. This decline in quality may result in the development of an embryo with chromosomal problems, which in turn increases the possibility of early spontaneous rejection of the pregnancy.

Along with these changes, women are more likely to suffer from complicated gynaecological troubles that can also affect fertility or the ability to carry a healthy pregnancy.

For those women who are finding it difficult to conceive, there are several options available, including the use of fertility treatment.

'For those women who are finding it difficult to conceive, there are several options available, including the use of fertility treatment.'

Chapter Three

How Age Affects You and Your Baby

For those women considering having a baby in their 30s or beyond, it can be very helpful to understand the risks both to yourself and the baby. It's helpful to also understand any complications associated with older mothers throughout pregnancy and birth, in order to try to prevent them occurring and having a more positive attitude to overcoming any hurdles faced.

It is true that many of these women will not experience any negativity at all during this time and enjoy the whole experience, as only the minority will find themselves facing challenges. Nevertheless, an awareness of the possibilities can be very useful.

Although you may feel young at heart and have the appearance of a woman far younger than your years, it is a fact of life that your body may be naturally changing without you being even the slightest bit aware of it.

For those of you who have delayed starting a family until now for sensible reasons that no one could argue with, your body still continues to conform to the aging process making the chances of complications during pregnancy and childbirth more of a reality than they may be to younger women.

The increased risk of birth defects

No parent wants to find out that there may be something abnormal with their growing baby, but unfortunately this is an issue that does arise more frequently in older parents than in the young.

For many of these, however, there is no obvious 'problem' with either parent or their families and the news can come as quite a shock.

Birth defect (or abnormality) is a term used to define an abnormality with the structure, function or metabolism of the developing child that will be present at birth.

These problems may result in either mental or physical difficulties, or in the worst cases the death of the child. It is, however, very important to remember that many babies born with health problems can have the problem treated successfully either as an infant or later on when they are more mature.

The risk of birth defects is a very real possibility for women conceiving over the age of 35. These defects may be the result of congenital developments of the foetus, chromosomal problems, genetic factors or even as a result of the unknown. Don't be too afraid though as many older mothers go on to have highly enjoyable pregnancies and births, delivering healthy babies every day.

Fortunately, there are some tests that can be carried out during your pregnancy to determine whether you are more at risk of carrying a baby with a birth defect. Although these are usually offered to all those over the age of 35, it remains your choice whether you undergo the test or not. Sometimes the guidance of your GP, midwife or other counselling service can help you make the right decision for your circumstances.

Lots of expectant mothers have the tests and find they are torn between the various options open to them, while others decline the tests deciding that the result would not influence their decisions over the remainder of their pregnancy. It is a very personal choice and something that normally requires a lot of thought and consideration of all the options.

'Lots of expectant mothers have the tests and find they are torn between the various options open to them, while others decline the tests deciding that the result would not influence their decisions over the remainder of their pregnancy.'

Why is there an increased risk?

For many families, the cause of the defect may remain unknown but there are strong links between some birth defects and chromosomal problems. For example, most people are aware that the risks of a child being born with Down's syndrome is higher in women over 40. This is thought to be because the quality of the eggs are poorer and the developing embryo is not as healthy as the cell division takes place.

How will I know if my baby is at risk?

Thankfully with modern technology the chances of finding out at an early stage if your baby may have a birth defect are higher than ever before. This does not mean that all abnormalities will be detected but for many, finding out opens up many more options. These options range from continuing with the pregnancy, to discussing with your healthcare providers whether the defect can be treated before the birth or how soon afterwards.

By taking blood tests, samples of amniotic fluid or tissue, or from sophisticated scans, it may be possible to assess the health of your baby or whether you are more (or less) at risk than previously thought.

The risks of having a baby with a possible birth defect may be explained to you before a test, whilst you are awaiting the results of a test or discussed after the results have been released. The decision of when this delicate subject may be approached varies between the practices of different healthcare professionals; many like to prepare couples for what may occur in the future, whilst others prefer to wait until a definite diagnosis has been achieved.

No doubt you will have several questions about the health of both you and your developing child, and you will be given several opportunities to discuss these over time.

'No doubt you will have several questions about the health of both you and your developing child, and you will be given several opportunities to discuss these over time.'

What sort of defects might my baby be at risk of?

The chances of a birth defect occurring raises with age, with those over 45 being at most risk; common defects include Down's syndrome, Edward's syndrome and Patau's syndrome. These conditions are all chromosomal in nature, each disorder is caused by an abnormality or anomaly affecting a different set of chromosomes with a different set of symptoms.

There are also risks of developing heart defects, spina bifida and hydrocephalous (water on the brain), although these risks are equally as possible in other pregnancies and are not just seen in older mothers.

Can I prevent the chances of a birth defect?

There are some things you can do to try to lessen the risk of birth defects. These include, but are not limited to, eating a well balanced diet, avoiding under-cooked or raw meats, taking enough folic acid in the months leading up to conception (a supplement can help), making sure general health and physical fitness is good, ensuring you know about your familial history and telling your GP of any illnesses in the family, and avoiding alcohol, tobacco and recreational drugs.

It is also important to make sure your vaccinations are up-to-date so that you are protected from certain illnesses that can cause problems with your growing baby. Equally as important is to avoid contact with people or objects carrying known infections such as German measles and toxoplasmosis (found in cat faeces among other things).

Pregnant women are not exempt of being at risk of flu, including swine flu. In fact there is a very small increased risk of miscarriage in those who contract flu, but with sufficient hygiene measures such as good hand hygiene and avoiding those who are known to have flu already, the risk is minimal. To find out if you are eligible for the swine flu vaccine, please speak to your GP or practice nurse.

By following these guidelines your chances of a healthy pregnancy and birth are increased, but some risks remain and many women will have already conceived with the developing embryo being at risk of some possible defects even before she was pregnant.

The increased risks of miscarriage

All women who are pregnant or about to try for a baby will be aware of the risk of miscarriage and the risk overall is one in every eight pregnancies (something that many people are quite shocked to learn). Unfortunately, this threat is more prominent for those in the older mother category. Many women in this age group do go on to have healthy, problem-free pregnancies, but as the risk is increased it is something you should be aware of so that you can act quickly should anything untoward occur.

What is a miscarriage?

A miscarriage occurs with the loss of a pregnancy before 24 weeks gestation. In most cases the miscarriage occurs very early on, often before the woman is even aware she is pregnant, with the majority of women miscarrying before the 12 week mark.

There are several reasons why a miscarriage may have occurred. Common reasons include the overall health of the mother, if the mother is a smoker or drug taker, if the mother has certain underlying illnesses and defects occurring with the growing embryo or foetus. Sometimes, not even the experts can give an explanation and it is simply down to Mother Nature.

Reasons why older mothers are more at risk

A large proportion of those who miscarry may find it is due to chromosomal problems with the developing embryo or foetus. Many studies have been carried out over the years to find out why the risk of chromosomal problems increases with age but this area is still not fully understood. It has, however, been shown that these problems do contribute to miscarriage, possibly as nature's way of preventing abnormalities in live offspring. It is thought that as the quality of eggs produced falls as we age, so too does the quality of any embryos that are created. When these embryos try to develop in the womb, they have more difficulty finding a secure environment than one that is healthier which may be the reason for a miscarriage.

There is also a possibility of links between having high blood pressure and diabetes and miscarriage. The chance of either occurring increases as we grow older, thus showing another possibility why older women are more likely to miscarry during the pregnancy.

Older mothers are also offered more extensive tests than their younger counterparts and occasionally these tests can increase the risk of miscarriage, often a fact that may contribute to the decision made by parents giving consent or non-consent to the test.

Can I prevent it happening?

In many cases the answer is no, you may not have been able to prevent a miscarriage even with the best intentions and pregnancy preparation.

Despite this, there are some schools of thought that suggest the mother may be able to lower her chances of suffering a miscarriage by taking some preventative steps.

Having a good diet in the months leading up to the pregnancy and during the pregnancy (especially the first trimester) is thought to have a very positive effect on the growing embryo. It is also recommended that drugs and alcohol are forbidden during this time (excepting medications prescribed by your GP) as many substances can have devastating effects on both baby and mother.

Making sure all your immunisations and vaccinations are up-to-date is also very important, especially if there is a chance you may be exposed to certain illnesses such as German measles.

Despite all these preventative measures, it should be noted that in the vast majority of cases a miscarriage cannot be prevented as the problems that may have caused or contributed to the miscarriage are almost definitely down to chance genetic conditions within the developing embryo or foetus.

'Having a good diet in the months leading up to the pregnancy and during the pregnancy (especially the first trimester) is thought to have a very positive effect on the growing embryo.'

Effects of miscarriage

It is an unfortunate and sad fact that the chance of miscarriage is significantly higher in those in the latter stages of their fertile years, regardless of whether they have conceived naturally or using fertility treatment. Those who have fertility problems are actually a little more likely to be at risk of miscarriage than those who conceive naturally.

The effects of miscarriage can be devastating and cause a great deal of emotional and physical distress. This is something that may need discussing before you decide to have a child, or whether you want to try for another pregnancy in the event of a miscarriage.

If you are worried about miscarriage or wish to discuss bereavement, please speak to your healthcare provider as soon as you can so that a referral can be made to the appropriate specialist team.

The increased risks of a complicated birth

The term 'complicated birth' can cause a lot of distress for women of all ages. Though research does tend to agree that older mothers do seem to be at risk of needing more intervention during the labour and delivery, it should be remembered that even those with the healthiest of pregnancies and backgrounds are still at risk of needing some additional help during this time.

You should try to understand the reasons behind further intervention as sometimes it may simply be to err on the side of caution rather than for an exact reason.

What is a complicated birth?

A complicated birth is determined as those that need additional medical intervention rather than a normal vaginal delivery. As all possible interventions are carried out in controlled environments, perhaps the expression 'complicated birth' is a little misleading and causes additional fear for the mother when she hears the term being used. In actual fact, these types of births are very common in all women and are simply a matter of assisted delivery, which is perhaps a gentler phrase to use.

Why am I more at risk of a complicated delivery?

There are many arguments why older women are more likely to need interventions during the labour or delivery. For the most part it is for your safety and to ensure the safe arrival of your baby.

One reason is because older women are more likely to suffer from high blood pressure and the chances of your blood pressure rising during labour and delivery are quite high, which may necessitate the medical staff to help the birth along. There is also evidence to show that the second stage of labour is longer in older women, perhaps because the womb and muscles are less able to manage this stage of labour and therefore assistance may be needed. Some people agree that occasionally it is the staff around you at the time of delivery that cause an intervention to be used. Staff may have a pre-existing

'A complicated birth is determined as those that need additional medical intervention rather than a normal vaginal delivery.'

perception that just because you are an older parent you will need assistance, and will therefore be increasingly concerned about the birth and may pass this stress on to you, causing your body to react.

Medical interventions during delivery

Statistics do seem to show that the chances of needing medical intervention during the labour and birth are more likely in older mothers. These interventions include the need to induce the labour, use an epidural for pain relief, the use of forceps or suction to assist the delivery or proceeding to a caesarean section.

There is also some evidence to suggest that the muscular contractions of the womb during labour are not as acute as those in younger women. This causes a longer labour, often requiring the use of synthetic hormones to induce and assist the contractions.

How a new baby affects your life

It is inevitable that having a new baby in your life is going to change things and often it can be easy to get swept away with your little one and forget how your life was before their arrival. It can also be very easy for parents to find that when the baby arrives, they unknowingly neglect areas of their life that were previously very important to them.

Although it may not seem like it at the time, babies really are only little for such a short period of time, and while it can be difficult juggling everything while being the best parent you possibly can, there are ways of maintaining your relationships with others and finding ways of continuing to be an individual. This is very important for your own psychological health as it can be easy to believe you have lost your identity.

Don't forget the birth is just the beginning

It can be very easy to get so wrapped up in the pregnancy that you forget this is just the first stage of a new life and lifestyle for your family. Once you have had the baby you will find that things have changed and life will never be the same again; all of a sudden you are responsible for a tiny, dependent child and almost everything you do for the first few years is determined by the baby.

You will probably find that your priorities change and what used to be so important to you is less so. You will no doubt have less free time and how you spend this time will certainly change. Even if you try to make every effort, it is likely that the activities you would previously have done in your spare time will become less important and this can include spending time with friends or family.

Your relationships with others

As you have less time and most of your actions are dictated by the needs of your baby, those shopping trips or lunches out will probably become less likely while the baby is very young. Unless, of course, you have a very supportive network of people who are happy to look after the baby so you can pursue your interests or have time by yourself.

Having less time doesn't have to be a negative aspect of having a family. Many people adapt to this by simply changing where they meet their friends or by inviting them to the house instead of going out.

If you were previously used to going out a lot in the evening, perhaps you could adapt to this by going out a little earlier so you can be home in time to get enough sleep for the next day.

With regards to the relationship between you and your partner, you may find that having a child brings you extremely close as a family unit and you work really well together running a home, managing finances and being together.

For others though, having a baby does alter things somewhat and being tired can often mean your relationship is for the time being, no longer a priority. It can be easy to fall into this way of life and start taking each other for granted or snapping at each other as the tiredness sets in. But please do try to remember

'It is inevitable that having a new baby in your life is going to change things and often it can be easy to get swept away with your little one and forget how your life was before their arrival.'

that together you wanted to start a family and it really is one of the biggest blessings in life. Try to find opportunities to spend time together even if you don't go out or do anything traditionally 'romantic'. You can still appreciate each other by cooking and enjoying a meal together, using massage to relax or just going out and having a long walk together. Finding time to be with each other and communicate is very important in keeping your relationship healthy. Remember too that just because you have a new baby, it doesn't mean that you must spend every minute of the day talking about the baby.

Having a baby does not mean your social life has to stop or your relationships with people change for the worse, it simply means you must adjust and alter the way you previously did things so that they fit in with your baby's needs.

Physical changes

Having a baby will probably leave your body in a slightly different state than it was prior to the pregnancy. While some women allow this issue to become a significant concern in their life, other people probably haven't even noticed that you have changed. The good news is that most of the after effects of pregnancy do not last forever and will ease as time goes on.

One issue that is not discussed too often in either pregnancy literature or by women in general is the subject of after pains. Some women are very lucky and do not suffer from any after pains following the delivery of the baby, whereas others, particularly those who had a vaginal delivery, may find them to be excruciating. These are temporary pains and occur as the womb contracts down to its previous size before pregnancy, and so is actually a good thing to happen. It can be encouraged by breastfeeding, but women who bottle feed may also suffer from these pains.

Fortunately, they normally subside within a week or two and decrease in severity as each day passes. They may be eased by taking paracetamol or other similar mild pain killers.

Another change to your body is the size and shape of your breasts. They may have swollen considerably during the pregnancy or when breastfeeding, giving you the cleavage you always dreamed of. But when breastfeeding subsides you may find they look a little deflated and you are dissatisfied with them. Don't worry too much as some good creams and exercises can often help lift your bust, making any sagginess less noticeable. It is also important to remember not to act too quickly in finding a permanent solution for sagging breasts such as surgery, as this may impact in the size and shape of your breasts in future pregnancies or whether you can breastfeed in the future or not.

Women are also concerned about their vagina following delivery, especially if they had a vaginal delivery, tore or had an episiotomy (a small surgical cut to the area between the vagina and rectum that eases the passage of the baby) during the birth. Common concerns are whether their sex life will be the same, will it hurt, will they look different and will their partner still find them attractive. The good news is that this area heals very quickly and often leaves no noticeable scarring or stitch marks, so it is very unlikely that your partner will be able to see any difference at all.

You can encourage good muscular tone by doing regular pelvic floor exercises. This will not only help with bladder tone but it may also help tighten the vaginal muscles, possibly giving you more sexual pleasure than before providing you do the exercises properly and regularly. Please ask your midwife, health visitor or practice nurse for more advice on how to successfully carry out pelvic floor exercises.

It is not just socially and psychologically that life can change, as there are certain physical changes that can occur too. Women may also find (especially those who have experienced problems with their monthly cycle and fertility) that when the initial period after the birth has passed that their cycle is a lot more regular and less painful than before.

Coping with parenthood

It is no secret that having a new baby will affect your life. However, even if in the first few months it may not seem like it, it is assumed that all parents will agree that having children enhances their life in ways they couldn't have expected.

For many older women, there is so much focus on the pregnancy and birth they forget to imagine and plan their life after the delivery, and many are surprised at how their life is affected.

It isn't a surprise to most that babies are tiring, especially if they are difficult to settle, take short rest periods between feeds and generally need a lot of attention. Although you may have planned for a baby for a long time and have felt in top physical health and wellbeing, the tiredness and lethargy can come as a surprise, often leading the parents to question why they left it a little later than others to have a baby.

You may find that many of your friends are just getting their independence back as their own children grow up and suddenly you are stuck at home surrounded by bottles, bibs and nappies. This can be quite a wake up call for some people, even those who have spent their entire adult lives planning for the time when a baby is part of the household. Unfortunately, this is true for people of all ages for various reasons, and perhaps now is the time to ask your friends for help and advice, or maybe you could try finding new friends who are also new but older parents. Remember, there are more women now having babies in the late 30s and 40s, so there is likely to be someone somewhere near you in the same position just waiting for a friend.

Summing Up

If you have been waiting a long time to start a family or have had difficulty conceiving, it can be very easy to become totally absorbed by the pregnancy, especially because healthcare professionals and literature highlight the increased risks of having a more complicated labour and birth. With this in mind, it is easy to see how some women are so focused on having a trouble-free pregnancy that they forget about what happens after. The pregnancy is only the beginning and the reality of having a baby to look after and a child to raise can come second in the list of priorities.

You life is about to change, hopefully bringing a lot of joy and happiness. It can be very useful to make sure you are aware of what is available in your local area to help you when you need it, or think about setting up a supportive network to make the early years that little bit easier.

Chapter Four

Advantages of Waiting Until Later

Finding out you are pregnant slightly later in life than others around you may or may not be a surprise. For many couples, the decision to wait may be part of their life-plan and something that has been an overall aim and they have worked hard to achieve. For others, it may be an unplanned but nonetheless very special surprise. There are in fact many benefits of delaying a pregnancy until your 30s or 40s which are all equally understandable.

Financial security

One of the most common reasons for delaying having a baby until you are slightly older is because of financial reasons. This is an extremely sensible option in today's society and, as good parents, we all want the best upbringing and opportunities for our children, many of which can be costly. Many people also find that even though they have anticipated being worse off financially when a baby comes along, many of them do not realise how great the financial change may be.

Of course not all couples leave starting a family until later because of money, and there are many families that are no better off in their 30s or 40s than they were in their younger years.

'One of the most common reasons for delaying having a baby until you are slightly older is because of financial reasons.'

Hidden costs of having a baby

There are so many hidden costs after having a baby that you previously had probably not thought of. Most parents-to-be are aware of the typical shopping list such as a steriliser, a cot, a pram, clothes and such like, but over the first few years the costs can really add up and before you know it your savings are dwindling and suddenly all those years of planning seem a bit pointless.

For example, small things like heating your home, the amount of hot water and washing you go through are likely to escalate. Also there are issues such as childcare, maternity leave entitlements and being able to fit a child seat in the car to consider. There are also things like bottles, nursing bras, bibs or other small items that are likely to need replacing very frequently as they get worn, stained and out of shape very quickly.

However, these expenses will be counteracted by the change in your lifestyle. For example, you probably won't be going out as often so money will be saved there, and if you're not going out, you will be less likely to need new clothes, shoes and accessories (apart from around the house things). This does not mean that life is going to stop, just that you will probably find that you want to stay in more often, are happy to be spending your money on your child and that your interests and hobbies change a little.

Getting help with the costs

Having a family will spread your finances slightly thin, but there are certain benefits you may be entitled to depending on your circumstances.

- Child Benefit is payable to any family that is bringing up a child or children under the age of 16 and is not dependent on income or status.

- At the time of print, this stands at £18.80 a week for the first child and £12.50 a week for any subsequent children. The payment can be either collected from a post office or paid directly into your bank account.

- Child Tax Credit is a monthly (or weekly) payment paid to the main carer of the child and is aimed at families with incomes of up to £58,175 (or £66,350 if one child is under 12 months).

- The amount offered depends on your individual circumstances and you will be assessed regardless of whether you are working or not.

- Working Tax Credit is an additional payment offered to those on low to middle incomes depending on your income, the hours you work and any child care costs.

These payments can be applied for by anyone, though this does not mean you will necessarily be entitled to any payments. Often those working full-time will find that they are better off if they drop their hours or change salary.

How to save

If you are worried about the financial implications that having a baby will bring, then there may be a few simple ways of making sure you are still able to stash some pennies away at the end of the month.

To start with, why not consider breastfeeding? Not only is this better for both baby and you but the amount of money saved over a six month period is quite substantial. A typical tin of formula can cost around £7.50 and you may need one and a half of these a week, so over a few months the saving is quite a lot. Couple this with the money saved on bottles and sterilising costs and you really will be making quite a saving.

Also becoming increasingly popular are washable nappies. Initially this may not seem very appealing, but for a small fee you can have the nappies taken away, laundered and returned in just a few days. Disposable nappies are not only bad for the environment but are also very expensive and may need to be used for around three years before the child is dry 24 hours a day.

If you are having difficulty making the decision about which type of nappies to use, it may be more realistic to combine the two and use disposable nappies when outside the home and washable when at home and near to laundering facilities.

Another great way of saving a few pennies is to take advantage of all the freebies that are available to new parents of young children. Many websites and magazines offer freebies or will reward you for sharing your opinions on certain products and these can sometimes be quite worthwhile.

'Many websites and magazines offer freebies or will reward you for sharing your opinions on certain products and these can sometimes be quite worthwhile.'

When you are bought gifts, especially clothing, please don't be afraid to ask for the receipt. Not only can you exchange the item for a more appropriate size, you may be able to swap the item for something that fits in better with the seasons. Most parents will tell you they have been bought clothes for the baby that have never been worn as by the time the baby fits into them, the season has changed!

You may also find that people have bought you clothes or gifts in duplicate or even that you don't really like; with the receipt you can exchange these for something you do like or get the money back and spend it on something that is needed, like nappies for example.

Avoiding financial mistakes

It can be tempting when shopping for a new baby to go overboard. The choice of baby furniture, clothes, nursery equipment and toys can be addictive and it is easy to get sucked into the 'while I'm here' trap. Please do try to stick to your shopping list and don't get caught up in something that will cost you dearly.

Don't worry about high chairs and baby walkers for now – these things are not needed for the first few months, during which time you may be offered one, see a bargain or find that you have changed your mind. Also unnecessary are things like baby changing units and nappy dispensers. Not only do they take up a lot of room, they cost a lot and will probably hardly ever get used. Much easier is to find a handy and accessible cupboard for nappies and then simply change the baby on the floor using a large soft cushion or quilt or a plastic wipeable changing mat that are portable and cost a fraction of the cost of the changing tables.

It can be very tempting when you go shopping to buy the latest and greatest that money can buy, after all your little one deserves the best. But how practical are these purchases? Does the new, all singing, all dancing pram you've just paid a thousand pounds for collapse small enough to fit in the car? Is it going to last the winter and the summer? Is it going to need a professional service or clean within the first few months? All these hidden costs add up so making that purchase could end up being a very costly mistake indeed.

'It can be very tempting when you go shopping to buy the latest and greatest that money can buy, after all your little one deserves the best. But how practical are these purchases?'

Always remember too that it is far better and productive to overestimate the costs of things than to underestimate and find you haven't enough money saved.

The best way to approach buying for a new baby is to write a list of items you would like and when any friends or family offer to buy something, show them the list and ask if they would like to either buy one of the smaller items or contribute to one of the more expensive pieces. Writing a list has other advantages too, as it gives you time to reflect on the item before you commit to buying it. Give yourself a few weeks or even months and keep looking at the item and others, until you have made a firm decision and are not making an impulse buy.

Financial independence

More women than ever are now finding their own financial independence and are relying on their partners less for support. If this is a good description of you, congratulations on making it independently, but please do not let your pride interfere when you are having a baby. The father of the child has an obligation to provide financially for any child he may have. You will be entitled to help and if you are not on good terms with the father, please do seek legal help for settling any financial issues.

Also good to remember is that when you are buying baby things, your partner may want an equal say in the purchases and will be as excited as you are in doing the shopping.

Your domestic arrangements

It can be easy to get so wrapped up in the pregnancy that the domestic arrangements are forgotten until the day you arrive home with your little one. Undoubtedly you will need to make some changes in the home and it can be very helpful to be prepared for this.

If you have waited for a baby because of financial arrangements or because you enjoy a nice home with good quality furnishings, having a little one can come as quite a shock. In the first few months you will probably find that the washing builds up, the living areas become more cluttered and as the baby grows, toys do not have a 'home' or that certain fabrics have become irreparably stained. This is all part of being a parent and something we all have to endure so it is far better to plan for these events than to let them overwhelm you.

Making a home

Even with a new baby, you can still enjoy your home and often having baby things around can make your house seem more homely than before. Try to enjoy the experience and make some simple alterations such as putting throws over your furniture, freeing up cupboard space in the kitchen or even changing the bedrooms about until you are satisfied you have sufficient room.

Safety is a big issue as well and things like electrical sockets, doors, windows and where you keep your cleaning products will no doubt need some thought. Remember that a crawling baby sees everything at almost floor level, so take a walk through your home and try to find ways of eliminating dangers before they become a problem when baby starts crawling. There are several inventions that can be bought quite cheaply for securing cupboard doors, sockets, windows and similar that will 'baby-proof' your home.

Your social life

Just because you are having a baby doesn't mean your social life has to end. You can still enjoy nights out while you are pregnant providing you are not subjected to smoky environments or drink alcohol outside the recommended limits. The only difference is that you may not actually feel like going out as much or you are simply too tired. Why not invite your friends round for a girly night in instead? This way you can enjoy their company without having to get ready, spend a lot of money on new clothes that you will only be able to wear for a certain amount of time, or have the worry of letting people down if you want to go home early.

After baby is born, it may take several months before you actually feel like establishing a social life again as you will be tired, you will be wrapped up in your little one and your time management skills may take a while to re-establish.

'Remember that a crawling baby sees everything at almost floor level, so take a walk through your home and try to find ways of eliminating dangers before they become a problem when baby starts crawling.'

During these times it can be more beneficial to try to socialise during the day rather than at night, which is a great opportunity for making new friends with other women who have just had babies. This can be done by taking advantage of any groups that are going on in your area, or why not create your own group yourself?

Creating a stable environment

It's not easy to create a peaceful and stable environment when your world has just been turned upside down by a new baby, but it is at these times that you can really make a good family environment and begin your journey as a solid family unit.

Communication is vital in establishing a good stable home and both you and your partner must make sure you communicate effectively to get through the difficult times when tiredness kicks in.

When you need to, ask other family members or friends for support, even if it is just for a short break when you and your partner can spend time alone together doing things that do not revolve around the baby, making these times as special as they can be.

Your overall health and lifestyle

Maintaining a healthy lifestyle can be quite a challenge when you are pregnant or a new parent, what with cravings, morning sickness and finding time for proper meals. But it is even more important for those in their 30s and beyond to take care of themselves during this time to avoid problems.

If you are finding it difficult, eat little and often or drink fruit juices or smoothies to make sure you are getting enough vitamins and minerals, try a multivitamin specially created for pregnant or new mothers.

'If you are used to keeping in good physical shape, you will probably find your pregnancy is a little easier as your body will cope better with the changes it will endure.'

Keeping in good shape

If you are used to keeping in good physical shape, you will probably find your pregnancy is a little easier as your body will cope better with the changes it will endure. If, however, you are frightened to take exercise for fear of damaging the baby then please do not worry too much. Obviously vigorous sports or contact sports are probably not such a good idea, but most forms of exercise can be altered to accommodate your change in circumstances and shape.

If you do not take much physical exercise, now is the time to start. Yoga classes or aqua-aerobics that are specifically targeted towards pregnant women are a fantastic way of improving your fitness, meeting people in the same situation and getting ready for the birth.

Whatever form of exercise you choose, please make sure you inform your instructor, coach, or training partners of your pregnancy so that provisions can be made to ensure your safety; if you are in any doubt, speak to your midwife or GP about your concerns.

Social habits – tobacco, alcohol and drugs

It goes without saying that in an ideal world, no one would drink too much, smoke or take recreational drugs, especially pregnant women.

There are many different sources of support for giving up smoking when you are pregnant. Many groups or helplines are specially created for the sole use of pregnant women and will give non-judgemental practical advice on how you can give up safely.

With regards to alcohol consumption, the general advice is that if you can live without it then this is the best way. However, if you really do miss having an occasional drink, you should not have more than two units, once or twice a week. Being in the older mother category, however, does mean you may carry a higher risk of problems, so most experts would advise that to minimise the risks, no alcohol should be consumed during the pregnancy and ideally in the months leading up to conception.

Recreational drugs are a no-no for everyone and unless your medication has been prescribed by your GP, then please do not carry on taking drugs in any setting as you may be severely risking the health of both you and the pregnancy.

Knowing you are ready

As already discussed, there are several reasons why people wait a few extra years before they start a family. But for some women, a baby was not part of their life-plan and not something that had previously been considered. Nature has a funny way sometimes of changing your plans and women approaching menopause often find that they suddenly feel the need to have a baby before they are unable to. This can come as quite a surprise to some women.

In many respects this is a very helpful experience as it proves you are ready and mature enough to cope with a pregnancy and a baby, rather than having to learn quickly if you find out you are having a surprise baby.

Other women and couples may have been thinking that they will have a baby one day but are unsure of when will be the right time and, for most, your body will tell you or has told you already.

If you do not feel quite ready, and are already pregnant, you may need to sit down with your partner or family and discuss what issues you do not feel prepared for and how you will address these. Perhaps you do not feel quite ready emotionally, physically or simply in your everyday life. Whatever the reasons, there are obviously things that need addressing during the pregnancy so that you can enjoy the rest of your pregnancy and your baby when it is born.

Maturity and confidence

There seems to be a general consensus that older mothers are better equipped for pregnancy and motherhood than young women as they are better able to cope emotionally, financially and are more at ease with themselves and their lives in general. This does not mean that younger mothers don't make as good mothers, or that older mothers won't struggle with a newborn, but broadly speaking, it does appear to be true. Older mothers do also seem more prepared to make sacrifices with their time and money, something which can be invaluable in the resulting happiness of your child.

Summing Up

Having a baby in your 30s and beyond has many advantages despite all the potential risks involved. These benefits are often what influence someone's decision to wait to have a baby.

The financial implications of bringing up a child are often highly underestimated by those who do not have children. Waiting until you are more financially stable or have saved sufficient amounts to help with the costs of looking after a child is a very sensible idea.

It is also a good idea to have achieved your targets in your personal life or career as this means you can dedicate more time and energy to your child rather than having to struggle finding a work-life balance or studying while you are a parent of a young child.

This does not mean younger women are less capable of raising a family but certainly, in many instances, these issues are extremely important.

'Routine tests are carried out to identify any potential problems that could arise during the pregnancy, and also as a way of detecting any existing conditions early on so that appropriate treatment can be offered.'

Chapter Five

Testing and Screening for Older Mothers

This is perhaps the most important chapter for expectant mums in the older age category as the issues of testing for certain disorders are often targeted at this age group.

Along with having the routine tests that are available to all pregnant women, you will be offered the chance to have more extensive testing to find out the health and welfare of both you and your baby.

Routine tests

Routine tests are carried out to identify any potential problems that could arise during the pregnancy, and also as a way of detecting any existing conditions early on so that appropriate treatment can be offered.

As well as the tests, you will be asked to give a detailed medical history of yourself and your family along with those of the baby's father to the best of your knowledge.

During your initial appointment, your midwife will probably want to find out your current weight and height to determine if you are over or under weight as this can sometimes mean you have an increased risk of complications later on.

Urine tests

Your urine will be tested at every scheduled appointment for the duration of your pregnancy. Even though your body has produced the fluid as waste, it still holds a wealth of information and as well as showing infections that may induce an early labour, it can also help diagnose pre-eclampsia which can be very dangerous for any pregnant woman. This condition can cause the mother's blood pressure to escalate steeply, sometimes to a very dangerous level that puts both the baby and the mother in jeopardy. Other symptoms include protein in the urine, blurred vision and vomiting; you will be tested for all of these conditions, but they can develop quite quickly, so make sure you report any symptoms to your GP if they occur.

Blood tests

When you have your first appointment with your midwife, you will be asked to provide some blood samples that will be sent away for screening. This blood will be tested for a variety of things including your red blood cell level, your blood group, your rubella status and certain diseases such as HIV, hepatitis B and syphillis. You may also be asked to provide another sample of blood at around 28 weeks to re-check your iron levels amongst others.

Dating scan

The majority of pregnant women know roughly when their last period was and will be able to give an educated guess as to how far along they are in the pregnancy when they first go to the midwife. From this date, you will be scheduled in to attend an ultrasound scan between 10 and 14 weeks (usually at 12 weeks). The purpose of this scan is to find out exactly how far along you are and what your estimated date of delivery is likely to be; this is done by taking several measurements of the baby.

Along with checking these measurements, the person performing the scan will assess the position of the womb, the cervix, the placenta, how many heartbeats can be seen and the general health of the baby, though a more detailed scan will be offered later for this.

Abnormality scan

An abnormality scan is offered at 20 weeks to carry out a very detailed assessment of your baby. All the major organs will be viewed and often measured, the skeletal structure can be assessed and any other problems can often be identified.

If any problems are detected, a second opinion is usually sought before a definite diagnosis is given. If you are told of an abnormality, you will have everything explained to you over time and all the possible options will be provided so that you can make an informed decision about what you wish to do with this information.

Amniocentesis test

Many women are confused as to what amniocentesis actually is and whether they need to consider the test. Before amniocentesis is offered you may be offered a screening test which combines data gathered from an ultrasound scan and results gained from blood tests. The results of these tests will not give you a definite yes or no answer of your baby having an abnormality, but it can help find out if you are more at risk.

What is it for?

The test is carried out to find out if there are any chromosomal problems with the baby which may indicate a congenital complication or highlight a risk of the child having Down's syndrome.

It is normally carried out after the 15th week of the pregnancy onwards, though if you leave it too long after this date your options may be more limited with regard to continuing with the pregnancy or not, if this is something you would consider. The results of amniocentesis are very reliable with most women obtaining a definite 'yes the baby does have a chromosomal disorder' or a definitive 'no' answer.

'An abnormality scan is offered at 20 weeks... All the major organs will be viewed and often measured, the skeletal structure can be assessed and any other problems can often be identified.'

Who is offered the test?

One of the most common groups of pregnant women to be offered amniocentesis are those who have certain hormones found in their blood and who are over the age of 35. These are frequently the two biggest risk factors and the two figures can be calculated to find out the degree of risk involved.

How is it performed?

Using an ultrasound scan, a very fine needle is passed into the womb, through the amniotic sac until the tip of the needle reaches the fluid surrounding the baby. From here a small amount of fluid is drawn off (about 20ml) which is then sent for testing.

As the needle is guided by the ultrasound, the foetus is unlikely to feel anything or be at any risk of injury.

There are, however, some concerns to be addressed, the procedure does carry a small risk of miscarrying the pregnancy either a few days or weeks later. It is this fact that makes making the decision whether to have the test such a huge issue for couples expecting a baby.

The rates of miscarriage following an amniocentesis are still part of an ongoing debate, though experts currently explain that around one in every 100-200 of tests carried out will result in a miscarriage. Whether this miscarriage occurs because of the test or would have happened anyway, is unknown.

You may have been told you have a slightly higher risk of having a baby with certain disorders and go on to have the amniocentesis only to lose a perfectly healthy pregnancy later. On the other hand, you may decide not to have the test and realise a lot later on, often after the birth, that your baby has some very serious complications that you were unaware of and unprepared for.

If you decide to have the test and achieve a positive result, your options will be discussed. You may want to continue with the pregnancy and make plans for raising a child with a possible disability, or you may wish to discuss other options with your healthcare provider.

It is a very personal decision and can be quite difficult to make. Your GP or midwife may be able to offer further advice or counselling on the subject before you make up your mind.

Chorionic villus sampling (CVS)

Not everyone has heard of the CVS test but it really is a very good and relatively safe way of finding out if your baby has any serious abnormalities.

To understand the test, a little bit of anatomical knowledge is probably needed. When the egg and sperm create an embryo, it splits into two halves, one will become the foetus and the other burys itself into the wall of the womb and grows into the placenta. This occurs early on in the pregnancy so the test can be carried out from about 10 weeks gestation. As the placenta is very young and is derived from the embryonic changes, it carries the same DNA as the embryo itself so any problems can be detected from this tissue.

What is it for?

The test is used to find out if a series of very serious genetic abnormalities are likely to be found in your baby. These illnesses and conditions may influence your decision as to whether or not to continue with the pregnancy, but can also be beneficial in preparing for a more challenging time if you do continue, giving you more time to prepare and adjust.

Who is offered the test?

The test is offered to those women over the age of 35 due to their increased risks of having a child with chromosomal abnormalities, to those with a familial history of genetic conditions and those who have had previous pregnancies that have highlighted the risk in the past.

How is it performed?

The test is performed using guidance from an ultrasound scanner. This time a fine needle is passed through the abdominal wall only. Instead of puncturing the amniotic sac, it is directed towards the placenta. When the tip of the needle passes into the placenta a tiny piece of tissue is extracted and sent for analysis.

Most women tend to agree that a CVS test doesn't hurt exactly, but can be quite uncomfortable. It has been compared to a rather invasive smear test and there maybe some abdominal cramping afterwards.

There is a very small risk of miscarriage involved with this procedure, so again careful consideration of whether you really want to know and take the risk is needed before you commit yourself. The miscarriage rate is thought to be around one in every 100-200, though again, it is not clear whether any of these miscarriages would have occurred regardless of the test.

Nuchal fold or translucency scan

It is possible that you will have this test carried out without even being aware of it and, in fact, most pregnant women will undergo the test regardless of their age.

What is it?

Assessing the nuchal fold, which is at the back of the baby's neck, is often the first method of detecting a baby to be born with Down's syndrome. The amount of fluid at the back part of the neck while the baby is in the womb is often more than in babies without the condition. This is not a definite diagnosis but may alert staff who can then offer the mother the option of having more extensive testing to try to clarify the likelihood of the baby having Down's syndrome.

Who is offered this test?

As mentioned already, the test may be performed on all pregnant women as part of the routine tests, but it may be more likely that older mothers are more aware of the test because of their own research, or have been told by staff that the nuchal fold will be examined.

What does it involve?

The good news about this test is that it is done at the routine 12 week scan that is offered to establish when your due date is likely to be.

Alpha-fetoprotein test (AFP)

Your midwife will probably ask you if you want to have the 16 week blood test during your antenatal session. This blood test is checking the AFP level in the blood, which is a hormone secreted from the foetal liver into the mother's blood.

What is it for?

The AFP test is usually performed to find out if the baby is at risk of having neural tube defects that can lead to spina bifida among other things. It can also test for some abdominal disorders and to a small degree, may indicate an increased risk of Down's syndrome.

There does, however, seem to be some controversy over the test as many produce false positive results; this is when a pregnancy tests as positive for a condition when the condition is not actually present. This might then lead to the mother having more extensive tests performed, such as amniocentesis, which do carry a higher risk of miscarriage.

The reasons for achieving a false positive result from an AFP test are wide and varied and may be down to something as simple a taking certain everyday medications, being unsure of your exact dates or the weight of the foetus to name but a few.

Who is offered the test?

All pregnant women will be offered the test and you will be asked to give explicit permission before the test is carried out.

It can be helpful for those who fall into high risk groups, but is still offered to other pregnant mums too.

How is it performed?

The test is carried out by your GP or midwife during one of your routine antenatal appointments (usually the one nearest to your 16 week date). It is a simple blood test and should be no more uncomfortable than a standard blood test taken at any other time.

Deciding whether to have the tests

Nobody can make you have the tests, and providing you are fully informed of all the advantages and disadvantages involved, your decision should be respected. It can be very helpful to spend some time thinking about your decision before you say 100% whether or not you wish to go ahead and often it is useful to seek advice from other sources to gain a wider perspective of the future.

Also important is to discuss the available options with your partner (or the baby's father if you live apart) as they too may be able to provide some insight into how they feel about the decision.

Weighing up the pros and the cons

It can be difficult to keep a clear head when you are making a decision about the health of either yourself or your baby and it can take a lot of time to find clarity in all the information around.

If you need to, why not make a list of all the pros and cons of having the tests and then leaving them for a few days before you return to them and reflect on your first thoughts?

'It can be very helpful to spend some time thinking about your decision before you say 100% whether or not you wish to go ahead and often it is useful to seek advice from other sources to gain a wider perspective of the future.'

Also quite helpful might be to seek advice from support groups or forums who are organised by those who have made the decision before and know exactly how you are feeling.

Do not feel pressured

Try not to let yourself feel too pressurised into making a decision one way or another. It can sometimes be very easy for friends and relatives to inflict their opinions on you and expect you to make the same choice as they would have. If you do seek advice from friends or family, try to choose those who you know will listen or provide a balanced argument rather than simply having a one sided opinion which might not be helpful.

Religious beliefs

If you have very strong personal or religious beliefs and you know that whatever the results of the tests they wouldn't affect your decision to carry on with the pregnancy, it may seem like a waste of time and money to undergo the tests when you already know what you would do in any outcome.

However, they can be useful in helping you prepare for an infant who may need extra special care depending on any condition, though the risks associated with some of the tests may outweigh your desire to find out. As you see, already there are many advantages and disadvantages to having the tests and only you and your partner can make the ultimate decision.

What happens next?

When you have had the variety of tests explained to you, you will be given some time to decide whether you want to go ahead and carry out the test. In addition to discussing things with your GP or midwife, it may be helpful to talk to others or carry out further research on the subject.

The majority of the tests do have to be carried out within a certain time frame so you must choose within this time scale.

It's your choice

It is not usually the routine tests during pregnancy that people worry about. It is normally those that are offered to the groups of women who are deemed to be more at risk of certain conditions.

It is in your interests to attend all the routine antenatal tests that are offered as this ensures the health and safety of you and the baby and can provide early alerts if intervention is needed.

For older mothers, there are more tests offered and sometimes careful thought needs to be given whether the tests are undertaken or not.

Though you may want someone to make these decisions for you, it is your choice and not something that you should feel pressured into.

Each person will have their own thoughts and reasons for either taking or declining the tests and though it may be hard, you shouldn't let others try to coerce you into choosing for you.

Changing your mind

You are entitled to change your mind at any time during the testing process, and this includes when the results have been issued to your midwife who will be able to disclose them to you. The only real exception to this is when you are having a scan and something abnormal is detected.

'It is in your interests to attend all the routine antenatal tests that are offered as this ensures the health and safety of you and the baby and can provide early alerts if intervention is needed.'

Summing Up

There are a variety of tests offered to pregnant women of all ages, but those over 35 will find they are offered more extensive tests too. This is because they are more at risk of having a baby with the possibility of a mental or physical disability.

Lots of these women decide they do not want to pursue the tests as they do not wish to find out if their baby is affected, while others are happy to undergo all the tests they are offered in the hope that they may gain as much information about their baby as they can so they can make decisions or have more time to prepare.

Ultimately, no one can decide for you whether you have the tests or not so it is vital that you give them adequate time and thought before making a final decision.

'You are entitled to change your mind at any time during the testing process, and this includes when the results have been issued to your midwife who will be able to disclose them to you.'

Chapter Six

The First Trimester

Congratulations on your pregnancy! If it wasn't planned, you may need a few days to get over the shock and adjust to the idea of being pregnant. If it was a planned event, however, you must be feeling extremely happy that your family will soon be gaining another addition.

The first trimester (weeks one to 12) of the pregnancy is a very important time for both mother and baby and your body is a hive of activity at the moment, even if you can't feel it.

During the first 12 weeks the fertilised egg grows into a baby, albeit very small. He or she will be almost fully formed by the end of this stage and will use the second and third trimesters to grow, mature and define its features and biological functions.

Your body now houses another human being and will be working very hard to provide all the baby needs to develop and will adjust in both size and shape as the pregnancy progresses.

Discovering you are pregnant

Finding out you are pregnant is bound to set your emotions on a rollercoaster, you may feel elated, shocked, full of panic or a mixture of many feelings and responses all of which are normal.

If your period is late, it is likely that you may have had an inkling of a pregnancy occurring or perhaps you thought you were in the first stages of the menopause, while others may have had a shock from finding out from the GP.

Although the media often portrays early pregnancy as a time of extreme happiness and euphoria, feeling slightly nervous, wondering how you'll cope or considering all of your options before you break the news to people is totally

'Your body now houses another human being and will be working very hard to provide all the baby needs to develop and will adjust in both size and shape as the pregnancy progresses.'

normal, especially if you weren't planning another child, already have a busy life or are struggling financially. In fact, many people would agree that it is sensible to sit back and take stock of the situation and explore all possibilities before you make any rash decisions.

Pregnancy tests

Whether the pregnancy was planned or not, a home pregnancy test is definitely the best way to confirm your suspicions. These tests work by measuring the level of a hormone called hCG (human chorionic gonadotropin) that is present in the urine of pregnant women. As the pregnancy becomes established the levels of hCG rise quite sharply which has enabled scientists to create tests that can even give you an indication of exactly how far pregnant you are. Once you have taken a test, you need to book in with your GP surgery as an antenatal patient.

The early symptoms

If you have had a pregnancy before, you may be very familiar with the early symptoms and for some this may be what gave away the pregnancy in the first place. But if this is your first pregnancy, you may not have noticed your body changing or think the changes are happening for other reasons.

There are many common signs of pregnancy such as a skipped period, nausea and sickness and breast tenderness along with some not so well known ones like spotting (light bleeding) when the embryo implants into the womb wall, experiencing a heightened sense of smell, having an aversion to certain foods or smells, needing to empty your bladder more often and becoming tired more quickly and more frequently.

Many of these symptoms can be overlooked in the first few weeks especially if you are busy, have an irregular menstrual cycle or have experienced emotional upset or stress lately, and many women either fail to notice or ignore these symptoms and blame them on something else.

If you have experienced even one of these indicators, please take a pregnancy test as you will need to tell your GP, make changes to your lifestyle and start considering your options if you are pregnant.

What you should be doing

There are so many considerations and alterations that have to be made in the first trimester to ensure the very best of health for both you and your baby. It can be helpful to embrace these changes as part of the pregnancy instead of feeling as though you are having to make sacrifices or change your life too much. After all, when the baby is born you will probably find your life changes quite dramatically even if it's not your first!

Diet

Your diet is hugely important during this time and often many changes have to be made to give you both the best start.

It is now very well known that the benefits of ensuring a good level of folic acid can help to develop your baby's spine and nervous system and can lessen the chances of the baby being diagnosed with conditions such as spina bifida or other problems of the spinal cord. As the spinal development requires a lot of folic acid and takes around 12 weeks to develop fully, it is recommended that women should ideally begin taking a folic acid supplement when they wish to conceive and continue to take it until they have reached or just passed the 12 week stage.

The supplements can be bought cheaply from a chemist or supermarket and are very small and easy to take. Alternatively, natural sources can be found in broccoli, sprouts, spinach and potatoes but to gain the required levels, an awful lot of these products will need to be consumed leading most women to rely on a supplement.

Exercise

Continuing with a regular exercise programme is very important and for most people the changes will be minimal. Obviously those who participate in high contact sports may need to alter their activity, but for most, swimming, jogging, cycling, aerobics and yoga can continue as normal as long as you tell your instructor or team mates that you are pregnant.

'Ensuring a good level of folic acid can help to develop your baby's spine and nervous system and can lessen the chances of the baby being diagnosed with conditions such as spina bifida or other problems of the spinal cord.'

If you don't take much exercise, now is the time to start. By improving your own lung function and increasing the capacity of your heart and circulation, your baby will receive an excellent supply of oxygen and nutrients. Activities such as swimming or yoga are perfect for pregnant women and the type of class can be tailored to your needs. You may find local classes that are specifically for pregnant women so not only will you reap the benefits of the exercise, you may meet other pregnant women with whom you can share your pregnancy and gain some good friendships.

Drugs, smoking and alcohol

As already mentioned, smoking while pregnant is an absolute no-no, so what better time to give up than right now for your family? It is not easy giving up a regular smoking habit, but there is so much help available in all areas of the UK that it is easier than ever before. There are even programmes and advice lines especially for pregnant women with advisors on hand to give you advice, not lecture you or condemn you for your habit.

Please speak to your GP for more advice on smoking cessation programs.

The subject of alcohol during pregnancy has been a hot topic of late and the arguments both for and against drinking alcohol during pregnancy have been much debated. In general, most experts believe that one or two units once or twice a week will pose no harm to your baby, but if you can live without it, then don't drink at all and keep the health or both you and your baby in tip-top condition.

Activities

There really is no need to worry too much about changing general activities apart from being more careful how you lift and move things either at work or at home. Try to encourage your leg and stomach muscles to carry the weight of objects or other small children and refrain from using your back to lift with as these muscles will take a lot of baby weight in later pregnancy and need protecting.

'If you don't take much exercise now is the time to start. By improving your own lung function and increasing the capacity of your heart and circulation your baby will receive an excellent supply of oxygen and nutrients.'

Sex can continue as normal, as long as you feel you want to, though tiredness and nausea may deter some women. If this does happen there are other ways of being close and intimate with your partner if you want to.

Telling your GP

Most GPs prefer women to have missed at least two periods before they book in as an antenatal patient as the chance of early miscarriage is high in the first weeks.

If you believe you are around eight weeks pregnant and have had a positive home pregnancy test then it is time to make that appointment. Don't forget there are some women who go to their GP thinking they are menopausal and find out they are pregnant, while others go thinking they are pregnant and find out they are in the early stages of menopause so it is really important to take a test at home before you go.

During the appointment your GP will take your pulse, blood pressure and ask about your general health while booking you in and will arrange for a midwife to visit you in a few weeks time.

Pregnant women who are over the age of 35 do carry a higher risk during pregnancy than younger women so your GP may want to carry out a more detailed assessment of your health status and ask more in-depth questions.

As there are additional tests and screening processes available to older mothers throughout the pregnancy, starting at around 12 weeks gestation, your GP may want to discuss these options with you either at your first appointment or your second.

If you have had previous healthy pregnancies and you are relatively fit and healthy, your GP may not be as concerned as they might be if this is your first pregnancy.

Spending some time researching issues surrounding age and pregnancy may be very helpful. A quick Internet search will produce some very interesting and valuable sites providing readers with many worthy articles and forums you can join giving you the chance to speak to others who have already faced these dilemmas and issues (see help list).

Sharing your news with others

Whether this is your first pregnancy or not, you may want to tell people you are pregnant as soon as you have had a positive test, while others like to wait until they have had their first scan at around 12 weeks when they have seen their baby themselves.

There is no right or wrong time to tell people you are pregnant as long as you feel ready and are happy that everyone knows your news. Often family members are told first although some couples like to wait until the pregnancy is fully established before they tell younger children in the home just in case a miscarriage occurs and this can be difficult to explain and cope with.

'During the first trimester your little baby is busy laying down all its foundations for the coming months and indeed for the rest of its life.'

If you are a considerably older mother, you may find that some people can be quite judgemental about your news; don't worry about other people. Allow yourself to enjoy your pregnancy and be assured in the knowledge that you are just as able to provide for your child as younger mothers or couples.

Some people may be concerned for your health and while this can be irritating, especially if you feel perfectly healthy, they are only showing concern and you may even find it comforting that people are concerned for you.

Your baby – the first three months

Although you will probably be unaware of what is going on inside your body, with the exception of the typical signs of pregnancy, the amount of activity occurring is actually quite staggering. During the first trimester, your little baby is busy laying down all its foundations for the coming months and indeed for the rest of its life.

In fact, during the first three months, your baby will develop almost all of its major functions, spending the remainder of the pregnancy fine tuning these building blocks and growing bigger and stronger every day.

From the moment the egg and sperm meet, a hive of activity begins inside you, drawing on your strength and nutrition for support.

Fertilisation and implantation

Whether your contraception failed or you planned to have a baby, the processes that take place are quite amazing and still continue to astound experts and healthcare professionals.

Ovulation occurs 14 days before your period starts and this involves an egg being released from the ovary. This egg is caught by the ends of the fallopian tube and is assisted down the tube towards the womb. At the same time the man's sperm that has been ejaculated enters the womb via the cervix and vagina. The strongest and healthiest sperm try to seek out the egg and make their way to the entrance of the fallopian tube. When the egg is found, the strongest sperm penetrates the hard shell of the egg and enters the centre; this process is called fertilisation.

After the egg has been fertilised it begins to divide into cells and small 'feelers' called chorionic villi help attach the divided cells to the wall of the womb, following which it tries to bury itself into the wall, a process called implantation. It is during these processes that the hCG chemical is made allowing for a test to be detected from the urine.

Foetal development

When the implantation phase has occurred and the cells are now firmly attached, your little development is now called an embryo. By week four some of the most important organs – the heart, spinal cord and brain – begin to develop and by week five the very first signs of a heartbeat occur. Week six allows for the first signs of a face to develop and by week seven the mouth, nose and ears can be seen along with tiny arms and the first signs of the legs.

Your baby continues to develop at an astonishing pace for something so small (around one inch by week nine) and he or she will start to move around and explore the environment, floating quite happily in the amniotic fluid that protects it. By week 11 the sex of your baby is established and he or she can now be classified as a foetus.

Foetal movements

Until your pregnancy has progressed to around week 16 you will not be able to feel any of the foetal movements occurring within, even though your little one is being very busy. He or she starts to move very early on (around week nine) but you will not feel these movements just yet.

Women who have had previous pregnancies will probably be able to feel movements earlier than those in their first pregnancy, but still not quite this early and you will have to wait for those first flutters no matter how hard you concentrate.

Your body – the first three months

Most women, with the exception of those who claim to simply 'know' when they are pregnant (some even believing they know the sex of the baby), do not feel pregnant until they can feel the baby move or start displaying a small bump.

Often it is the symptoms of pregnancy that give it away. These symptoms commonly include sickness or nausea (not just in the morning), sore breasts, increased frequency in urination, tiredness, feeling faint or dizzy, a sudden aversion to smells or foods that previously didn't bother you, a sensitivity to heat or feeling hotter than normal, heartburn and mood swings. It is not uncommon to experience all or none of these, so do not worry if you find yourself identifying with all of the mentioned symptoms or none of them as your pregnancy is still likely to be perfectly healthy.

If, however, you are frequently sick you must make sure you are taking plenty of fluids to avoid dehydration. Also important is to make sure you haven't got a urine infection so see your GP if your frequent urination is accompanied by any of these symptoms – lower abdominal or kidney pain, a burning sensation, taking a long time to start passing water or if your urine is darker or more cloudy than normal.

Your changing body

It is not uncommon for some subtle bodily changes to occur, many of them unnoticeable to you. These can include a slightly distended (swollen) abdomen, your hair and nails becoming more glossy than previously (or indeed they may appear more dry and fragile than before) and also your breasts may change.

Breast changes

Many women find their breast tissue becomes very tender in the first trimester. This occurs as they prepare to become the main food source for your baby and the milk ducts contained within get ready for this event. They may appear larger, more lumpy and may even develop stretch marks or change colour slightly; this is totally normal and in fact is a sign of a healthy pregnancy.

Your nipples may also change somewhat during this time and may darken, become more prominent and the areola (the area around your nipple) may enlarge and deepen in colour. Some women like these changes while others aren't keen. These changes can be temporary, with the nipples and areola returning to their normal state after the pregnancy or when breastfeeding ceases, while for some the nipples may retain some of the enlargement and colour changes permanently.

If you already have children, the changes may be minimal, especially if they happened in previous pregnancies and didn't return to 'normal' afterwards.

As women age, some find that their breasts enlarge slightly and drop a little too, so again the changes might not be as noticeable compared to those who are experiencing their first pregnancy or are a lot younger.

'Commonly called morning sickness, pregnancy related sickness can occur at any time during the day or night and can come on very quickly and pass equally as quickly.'

Tiredness

Feeling tired during the first 12 to 16 weeks is a very common occurrence and some women find this difficult to cope with, especially if they have other children in the house keeping them busy. This tiredness will pass as the pregnancy progresses, so bear with it and try to rest as much as you can. If you have a partner, now is the time to ask for a little extra help with the household chores or childcare responsibilities.

It can be helpful to eat little and often to try to keep energy supplies up rather than having your usual three meals a day. Several smaller meals or snacks may help supplement your energy and making sure you are drinking enough will be helpful.

Women who are very busy may have to alter their lifestyle a little to make these changes, but you will reap the benefits in the long term.

Cravings

Although they aren't experienced by everyone, cravings can come along at any time. Some are rather strange and others are relatively normal. They may or may not have happened in previous pregnancies, but as long as they are not harmful, they will pose little problem to you and you can indulge yourself a little bit.

It is possible, however, to suffer from 'pica', otherwise known as non-food cravings. These do carry the potential to be harmful as often women feel strong urges to inhale petrol or paint fumes, ingest toothpaste, washing powders, soap or other cleaning products, to name a few. Of course a craving can take any form, so if you wouldn't do it in your normal, everyday life, or know it is harmful to your body in any way, please try and refrain from giving in to it. If you really feel you are struggling to control your cravings, or suffer from a very unusual craving, please speak to your midwife for further advice.

Keeping a diary of your pregnancy and documenting things like cravings can make a very good keepsake of the pregnancy, and may raise a few chuckles in years to come when you share them with your children when they are older or having babies themselves.

Bowel, bladder and pelvis

During your pregnancy, nearly all of the activity is going on in the pelvis so it is to be expected that the organs in this area will be affected. Finding you are a little constipated is normal and you can make changes to your diet to try to avoid this, which also helps to prevent you straining when passing a stool and can help to avoid the occurrence of haemorrhoids in the future.

You will also find that you need to empty your bladder more frequently, both at the beginning and at the end of the pregnancy. As the womb grows and changes position accommodating the growing foetus, your bladder may have a smaller capacity than before and also may feel some stimulation from the baby and the enlarging pelvic organs and vessels. Although this can be annoying, especially if you are being disturbed during the night or while at work, it is all part of the pregnancy and you must make sure you continue to drink plenty and stay hydrated. It can be helpful to limit the amount of fluids you take in the evening as this can help lessen the chances of needing the toilet in the night, but you must make up for these fluids during the day.

Managing sickness

Commonly called morning sickness, pregnancy related sickness can occur at any time during the day or night and can come on very quickly and pass equally as quickly.

Most women simply grin and bear it and, for almost all, the early weeks are the only time when nausea and sickness are a problem. Some do experience extreme sickness throughout the pregnancy and this is called hyperemesis gravidarium. Your GP or midwife will be able to help you alleviate the symptoms or treat you as necessary.

'Keeping yourself healthy is absolutely vital at this stage as you prepare for the birth. Your baby is now growing quite quickly and will be taking a lot of nourishment from the placenta and therefore you.'

Summing Up

The first trimester of your pregnancy is a very exciting but unnerving time. While there is a multitude of activities going on inside your body, your outward appearance often remains unchanged and it can be difficult to understand why you feel so tired or irritable when there is nothing obvious going on.

There are many things you can try to alleviate the less pleasant symptoms of pregnancy, though these do not work for everyone and sometimes they simply have to be endured until they pass.

As the trimester ends and you enter the next phase, the symptoms usually become fewer and fewer and your body starts displaying the more common characteristics of pregnancy.

Chapter Seven

The Second Trimester

Reaching the second trimester (weeks 13 to 26) is often considered to be a landmark in a pregnancy, mainly because the chances of miscarriage decrease quite sharply at this stage. As the risk of miscarriage tends to be higher for older mothers, it is understandable to feel relief at getting to this stage.

It is during the second trimester that many of the tests offered to older mothers are carried out so although the physical symptoms may have worn off, there may be some very emotional times and difficult decisions to make.

Keeping yourself healthy

Keeping yourself healthy is absolutely vital at this stage as you prepare for the birth. Your baby is now growing quite quickly and will be taking a lot of nourishment from the placenta and therefore you. As you approach the end of your pregnancym you may not have the energy to continue with the same level of activity as you would normally. Therefore, it is important to remain active now to stay fit and healthy and improve the chances of having a smooth birth with no problems.

Being pregnant does not mean you have to stop everything and sit down and sleep all of the time, in fact it is quite the opposite. If you have had no problems with your health and have not been advised by your GP to take things easy, continuing with your normal routines (with the exceptions of heavy manual work and some sports) shouldn't be a problem. Most women find that they begin to get their energy levels back around weeks 14 to 16 and are more able to resume a normal level of activity after the initial symptoms of pregnancy start to wear off.

However, it is important to listen to your body and this often means trying to get a little more rest and sleep and taking regular breaks throughout the day. Older mothers in particular tend to report feeling a little more tired than their younger counterparts, possibly due to the pressures of having a career or simply because they are a little older and less vigorous in their activities to begin with.

There are some safety tips to staying healthy in the second (and third) trimester. For example, in the past, women may have been excused for not wearing their seatbelt when travelling in the car but this is no longer the case. Even though your expanding tummy may feel like it won't fit the seatbelt or feel uncomfortable, it is essential that you wear it placing one strap above the bump and one under it.

Another small tip is to make sure you visit the dentist during this time. Pregnant women are entitled to free dental care in the UK and this is because being pregnant can play havoc with your teeth and gums. Both you and your dentist have to be more vigilant in making sure that your oral hygiene doesn't suffer or that problems are spotted early on.

Exercises for pregnant women

In general there are only a few sports or exercises that should be avoided while pregnant and a little common sense is usually enough to tell you what these are. Obviously sports that involve a lot of direct body contact or a lot of manual handling are probably not a good idea, while high impact exercises may have to be toned down to adjust to your change in circumstances.

As long as you tell your instructor, coach and team mates of your condition, then many activities can be continued almost as normal unless your body shows signs that you must stop.

If you feel too tired to exercise, then change your usual activity to something less energetic such as yoga or gentle but regular swimming. Exercises like these will keep your muscles toned, help you regain your figure after the birth and may actually contribute to having an easier and less prolonged labour.

'In general there are only a few sports or exercises that should be avoided while pregnant and a little common sense is usually enough to tell you what these are.'

It is also important to make sure you incorporate a good warm-up and warm-down with your exercise plan as your muscles need this time to adjust, and you will lower the risk of injury if sufficient time is provided to make sure your body is ready to exercise.

Listen to your body

No one is experiencing this pregnancy except you, so it is important to listen to what your body is telling you.

If you feel the need to rest, make sure you make the time for frequent rest periods, even if you have to discuss this with your employer. Likewise, if you need to take shorter but more frequent breaks, you should try to negotiate with your employer ways of arranging your scheduled breaks or temporarily changing your working patterns.

You may also find that you are becoming increasingly uncomfortable as your shape changes and your size grows. As your baby grows you may find it uncomfortable sleeping or sitting in certain positions and may have to adapt to this. Perhaps you need to use a chair at work or exchange the normal heels for flatter shoes; again you may need to explain this to your employer if you are required to wear a set uniform for work.

Pregnancy and work

It is at this stage that you must think about and start arranging the length of maternity leave you wish to take. Each employer will have their own policy regarding maternity and paternity leave, though there are laws issued by the government that must be adhered to. It is always a good idea to look into the law and compare it against your employer's policies regarding this subject.

As an employee you are also obliged to tell your employer of being pregnant 15 weeks before your baby is due. Part of this obligation is so your employer can carry out a risk assessment of your duties and working environment and plan staffing issues if you are taking maternity leave. You are also obliged to tell them of your plans and put this in writing. Please see www.direct.gov.uk for further guidance.

Foetal developments

At the beginning of the second trimester (week 13) your foetus is about the size of a tomato, has already laid down most of the building blocks for life and is now starting to take the shape of the baby he or she will become. Having spent the last three months developing the major organs and forming its little body, it is now practically fully formed and will spend the remainder of the pregnancy maturing.

He or she now actually looks like a baby with the body becoming more in proportion to the head, with legs and arms growing, making him or her more human.

The ears are beginning to take shape and already the gentalia may be recognisable on a scan. The internal organs are all settling into the correct anatomical place and important hormones and chemicals are being made and released.

Braxton Hicks

Braxton Hicks are a somewhat strange phenomena to many women, as they come in a variety of strengths, frequencies and sometimes apparently not at all (though experts believe this is because the mother is either too busy to feel them or does not recognise them when they do occur).

GPs believe that these usually spontaneous and random contractions are your body's way of practicing for the labour and of allowing the womb to change shape.

They feel as though the womb is tightening almost to a proper contraction which can be quite alarming at first, especially if you do not know of their existence.

The tightening usually lasts anything from a few seconds to a full minute before it relaxes. This can happen just once or twice or several times a day for the second half of the pregnancy.

They are mostly nothing to worry about, but, they can become stronger and last longer towards the end of the pregnancy, and when your contractions do start for real it can be quite easy to initially mistake them as frequent and strong Braxton Hicks contractions.

Baby's growth and development

During the second trimester, your baby makes the transition from being less likely to survive if born before the age of around 24 weeks (known as a 'non-viable' infant), to carrying a far greater chance of survival if born after this date (otherwise known as a 'viable' infant). He or she is still very busy in the womb and will be moving freely around in the amniotic fluid twisting and turning quite happily.

Although your baby has been able to hear some amount of noise for some time, such as your heartbeat or muffled external sounds which have been softened by the amniotic fluid, he or she now has a more acute sense of hearing and will be able to listen to quite a lot of what is going on in the outside world. In fact, some babies actually 'jump' or become startled by sudden or loud noises which you may be able to feel. Do not worry, these incidences will not harm the baby and actually show that your little one has a keen sense of hearing.

It is during this stage that your baby will be starting to create a layer of very fine hair all over the body. This is called lanugo and its purpose is to stop his or her delicate skin from being damaged by being suspended in the amniotic fluid for so long.

Believe it or not, your baby is already beginning to make his or her first stool which is passed soon after birth and is called meconium. This sticky substance is already accumulating in the bowel, even at this early stage.

During the later stages of the second trimester your baby is really beginning to explore the environment around and may have discovered the umbilical cord, his or her toes and may even suck a thumb. Even at this stage, he or she will react to anything that goes near the mouth and this is a good sign as it may help with establishing feeding (particularly breastfeeding) after delivery.

During the last weeks of the second trimester, your baby has started to lay down a small fat layer, adding to his or her weight to make them more robust in preparation for being born. The eyes are starting to mature and he or she will be able to open the eyes and sense their first experience of sight, albeit very compromised.

At the end of the second trimester your baby is around 34 cm in length (crown to rump) and will continue growing now at quite a steady but rapid rate.

Finding out the sex of your baby

Finding out the sex of the baby is not something all couples want to do, nor is it offered in all hospitals.

For many, it is seen as a good way of planning ahead and organising bedrooms, clothes and names or even just out of curiosity. For others, the surprise of finding out at the birth is something to be looked forward to.

This is a highly personal decision and only you can make it. Do remember though that not all hospitals or healthcare professionals will be permitted to disclose whether they can tell the sex of the baby or not, this depends on their local policy. Nor might it be possible to actually see the sex of the baby as the baby's position in the womb may prevent the genital area from being seen. If you have a healthy pregnancy and do not need any more than the required number of scans, you may not find out until the baby's birthday despite your request.

It is worthwhile discussing this option with your partner as you may have differing opinions on the matter and without talking to each other, a surprise could be ruined for one of the party during the scan. Some couples who do find out the sex also like to keep this information to themselves until the birth, while others like to share the information with family and friends as soon as they find out. The choice is totally yours as to what you do with the information providing your request can be fulfilled.

'During the last weeks of the second trimester, your baby has started to lay down a small fat layer, adding to his or her weight to make them more robust in preparation for being born.'

Your changing body

It is almost inevitable that your body is going to change quite significantly during pregnancy and as a result of childbirth (especially vaginal deliveries) sometimes these changes are unfortunately permanent. Many women look forward to the changes as they like to relish the whole concept of pregnancy, while others dread the transformation and hope they are not too badly affected.

Unfortunately, the changes that occur are often not preventable and you will have little control over how badly you are affected, and more often than not they really begin to kick in during the second trimester.

The possible changes that could occur are very extensive but the most common ones are getting stretch marks, enlarged breasts, weakened bladder, developing piles, thinning hair and weight changes.

In some instances a healthy diet and exercise regime can help to lessen the effects or even help your body recover to its former state in the months after delivery, though this is not the case for everyone.

Decrease in early symptoms

Plenty of women report that one of the best parts of the second trimester is when the early symptoms begin to decrease. GPs believe this is because by the second trimester, all of baby's major organs and functions have been established and the remainder of pregnancy is spent maturing and growing the baby within.

You may find that as your nausea decreases, your appetite is boosted and you could eat more than ever before. This is normal and is your body's way of telling you that baby is growing. Make sure that you do not satisfy this appetite with too many sugars and fats as these will have little benefit to your health and will leave longer lasting consequences such as weight gain, a secondary craving for salt and may put your dental health at risk.

'Not all hospitals or healthcare professionals will be permitted to disclose whether they can tell the sex of the baby or not, this depends on their local policy.'

You may also find that you need to urinate less often as your baby is now growing into your abdomen instead of being sat very near to your bladder. This is often a huge relief as you can now get a proper night's sleep without too many toilet interruptions.

Also common is to find that your mood improves and you are less irritable. Some women do not notice that they have become quite ratty in the first few weeks but often their partners will testify that they have! Now, however, you will probably find that you are happier, have more energy and are more alert than in previous weeks.

Weight gain

Weight gain is a very natural part of pregnancy and is a healthy sign that your baby is growing well. There is an awful lot of pressure on women these days to put on little weight and regain their pre-pregnancy figure very quickly after the birth. This is not healthy for most women and looking after your baby's welfare is far more important than fitting into a pair of skinny jeans.

Most women put on around two to two and a half stone during the nine month pregnancy, much of which comes towards the end when baby is undergoing a rapid growth spurt before the birth. These figures are for an average women so there is a chance you will put on less or more than this (especially if you are carrying more than one baby).

It is likely that your midwife will calculate your body mass index (BMI) during your booking appointment. This is a calculation of your height-to-weight ratio. By doing this and measuring your BMI later on, he or she can assess whether you are gaining enough weight during the pregnancy. This is often a good indication of your baby's development and can help indicate whether you are carrying a healthy amount of fluid around the baby.

If you were already overweight before the pregnancy, please do not try to diet during this time as your body and your baby's health may be at risk of not getting sufficient nutrients to withstand a healthy pregnancy. It is far better to try to eat healthily with plenty of fruit, vegetables, dairy and fluids rather than try to follow a particular diet.

Equally as important is to make sure you do not just eat 'comfort' foods during the pregnancy or use the time as a chance to overeat. It is true that you will probably be more hungry than before, and a few little treats won't do you any harm at all, but eating sweets, chocolates, puddings and large amounts of fats or carbohydrates is not going to do you any favours, so try to limit these as you would in your normal day-to-day nutritional intake.

Breast changes

Your breasts will undergo many changes in the second trimester, some of which women (and their partners) enjoy very much, though others are not so pleasant.

To begin with you may find that they become more sensitive than usual. This is something that often women do enjoy, but if they become extremely sensitive, even the lightest of touch can make them feel very tender and not a nice sensation at all.

Other changes include more prominent veins. As your breast tissue gets ready to produce a supply of milk for a newborn, the blood supply increases to accommodate this and the additional breast tissue you may develop. Your veins are likely to be a lot more noticeable especially in very pale women. Do not worry, they will almost definitely return to their normal appearance after breastfeeding has ceased (or your milk supply has diminished if you choose to use formula).

Also likely is a noticeable change to the nipples. Not only are they likely to become larger and more prominent, staying erect for longer periods or all the time, but the area surrounding the nipple itself will darken and enlarge too. Often the enlargement is quite marked and surprises a lot of women. The breasts themselves are also likely to swell, and now is a good time to start thinking about getting some new bras. Do not spend too much on them as two or three firm cotton bras should be enough to last you through to the end.

Foetal movements

Most women look forward to feeling the first movements of their baby as this is often when they start to 'feel' pregnant and now have some evidence of being pregnant especially if they are not showing any bump yet.

If this is your first pregnancy, you may not feel the movements until later on in the second trimester. They can initially be quite difficult to identify as they are unfamiliar and often not noticed or blamed to be wind. It can also be a little difficult to say whether the sensation was definitely the baby if the movements are primarily infrequent as they often are.

Do not worry if you haven't felt any movements until the end of the second trimester as some women (and babies) take longer, and any concerns can be addressed during your next scan.

'The first tiny movements of your baby have often been likened to the sensation of a butterfly fluttering its wings in your tummy.'

Flutters

The first tiny movements of your baby have often been likened to the sensation of a butterfly fluttering its wings in your tummy. Other women have described this sensation as a gentle 'popping' or like having wind moving through your abdomen.

These are in fact the tiny stirrings of your small baby who, although they have probably been very active before the second trimester, is now big and strong enough to make their presence known to their mother.

These movements are very special and something that should be treasured as, at that point in time, you are the only person experiencing the movements that are happening.

As your pregnancy progresses you may also be able to feel your baby's hiccups which may present as regular jumping or jerking sensations.

Was it a kick or not?

After the initial fluttering that may or may not have passed you by, you will inevitably feel some stronger movements as your baby's limbs begin to stretch out more. These can sometimes be quite strong and make you jump, especially if you are very relaxed. The movements can also sometimes be seen on the outside of the abdomen as the baby gets bigger. Again, these movements can still be very occasional at this stage so there is no need to be alarmed if you don't feel them every day.

In the past, women were encouraged to keep a kick count log of the baby's movements. Experts generally agree that this is not good practice these days as it causes unnecessary worry for both the parents and health professionals because, although the baby is often very busy inside the womb, the movements are not always noticed or strong enough to register with the mother. Baby kick counts are much more useful towards the end of the pregnancy when the movements are a lot stronger, more regular and you learn your baby's sleep and wake patterns.

Keeping a diary

Keeping a diary or record of your pregnancy is a very good idea as it is a very special time and something that makes a very good keepsake for both you, your partner and your children to reflect on in the future. Memorable occasions like feeling the first movements or funny occasions when the kicks occur can make ideal diary entries. Describing how you felt when you first experienced the movements or times when your partner was first able to feel the kicks are very special events that are extremely personal to each couple, and are also nice to reflect on if you have any further pregnancies as a comparison.

Summing Up

The second trimester is probably the best stage of the pregnancy as this is the time when your energy levels return, your symptoms (if you had any) have lessened and you really start to look pregnant. Also a big relief is to have passed the crucial 12 week mark which indicates quite a decline in your chances of miscarriage, which is something that is usually a fairly big issue for older mothers.

Around the mid-stage of the second trimester you will start to feel baby moving around in your womb, thus confirming the reality of the pregnancy and it can be a very special time for most mothers-to-be.

The difficult part of the second trimester is the decisions you have to make regarding the different tests and scans that may be offered to you. Because of your increased risks of birth defects or abnormalities you will be asked if you want to determine the chances of being affected. These decisions are often very difficult to make and take a lot of thought and discussion from both parents.

Chapter Eight

The Third Trimester

The final stage of your pregnancy, the third trimester (weeks 27 to 42), is full of excitement and often worry as the birth itself and meeting your little one looms in the none too distant future. All the planning and experiences of the past year are about to culminate in one of the most important events that is likely to happen to you.

Living with your bump

Adjusting to an enlarging tummy can take some getting used to, and they come in all shapes and sizes and may be quite high or settle low on your body.

It will get bigger day by day with you barely noticing, and even the most basic of everyday tasks may need you to eventually adapt your living environment.

For some women, the changes can begin very early on especially if you are carrying twins or more, whereas others may have to wait until they are around 20 weeks before they start to feel their clothes getting a little tighter.

Sleeping

Sleeping during pregnancy can be a whole new experience what with having to get up to use the toilet more often, feeling the heat more easily and trying to get comfortable with an expanding belly, but there are some things you can do to try to make yourself more comfortable.

It may help to change the nightwear you sleep in and exchange your usual night clothes for loose fitting nighties or pyjamas with an elasticated waist. Some women may actually prefer to sleep with no clothes on as this is more comfortable.

As your bump gets bigger you may find it uncomfortable to sleep on your front or worry about squashing the baby inside. It is generally agreed to be safer to sleep on your left hand side if you can, especially towards the end of the pregnancy, as this prevents major blood vessels being compromised by the added weight.

Also helpful is to buy a few extra pillows and position them under your tummy if you are laying on your side, with another between your knees. This gives additional support and helps distribute your weight evenly.

'It is generally agreed to be safer to sleep on your left hand side if you can, especially towards the end of the pregnancy, as this prevents major blood vessels being compromised by the added weight.'

Some women report that they prefer to sleep alone during the pregnancy as they sleep lighter and cannot get enough room with their partner beside them. If you need to, try to spend time sharing the bed and having some degree of intimacy if you wish. Explain to your partner that you need a good night's sleep in a cooler room and make alternative arrangements, reassuring your partner that this is a temporary measure.

Clothing

The issue of maternity wear is something that most women don't pay much attention to until they need it. They are generally very expensive to buy brand new, with many shops choosing to offer a small selection of maternity wear either within their 'normal' shops or online. You may find that unless you live near a large shopping centre, suitably priced maternity clothing is unavailable and you have to look further afield, online or rely on friends passing their old clothes to you.

As you will only be wearing these clothes for a few months, it makes little financial sense to buy a whole new wardrobe, whereas careful selection of a few sensible items such as jeans, black trousers and tops that can be worn during the day and at night with accessories makes much more sense.

If you know someone who has recently had a baby and is a similar size to you, why not ask them if they kept hold of their maternity clothes and offer them a little financial reward for them? The chances are that they will still be good quality as the previous owner will have only worn them for a few months too.

It is also a good idea to look online as there are some sites offering a swap shop for maternity clothes or you can simply buy the goods at a much lower price than other retailers can offer.

If money is not an issue for you, then there has never been so much choice available as there is today. Gone are the shapeless dresses and dungarees and in replacement are designer outfits that could have come straight off the catwalk. Have a good look round and make your selections carefully and try to choose comfort over style as you will feel more uncomfortable and warmer as you get bigger, particularly in the middle of the summer.

Getting comfortable

Getting comfortable even during the day can be very tricky, particularly as your pregnancy progresses. You might find you need to take more breaks, choose a different chair to sit in, alter your normal clothing or even change your footwear.

It is advisable that you avoid wearing high heels for long periods when pregnant. Try to find shoes that do not need to be fastened (you may be unable to reach later on) and ones that are soft enough to allow your feet to spread out if they swell.

It may also be helpful, especially if you are suffering with an aching back or sciatica, to carry a lumbar pillow for when you are seated or driving as this offers additional support to your spine.

Bathing

When you have had a hard day and have an aching back, there is often nothing quite so relaxing as a hot bath in peace and quiet.

Bathing is a great way of unwinding and also offers you the perfect opportunity for getting to know your changing shape and spending some quality time thinking about your future as a parent. It may also give you some alone time with your baby who may respond to your voice or movements when you are in the bath, allowing you to see their movements with no clothing in the way.

There are, however, some tales that suggest a bath should not be too hot while pregnant. While the evidence is a little vague on the effects of very hot bath water on your baby, healthcare professionals generally agree that water should be warm enough to be a comfortable and a relaxing experience, but not too hot that you start sweating or turning too red. The reason for this is more for your safety as the risk of your blood pressure dropping sharply, especially when getting out of the bath, is quite high and may cause an accident and endanger both you and your baby.

If you really do enjoy a hot bath and feel as though you simply must have hot water, try opening a window to let the steam out and to keep your face cool while relaxing.

Personal hygiene

There is no need to alter your personal hygiene when you are pregnant unless you feel you want to. For example, many women find they feel the heat more, especially at the end of the pregnancy, and sweat more, requiring them to want to wash more frequently or bathe more often. There is no problem with this and it can be a good way to make sure you have some relaxing time during the day.

The only issue that you may need to be cautious of is paying too much attention to your groin area by cleaning too thoroughly. There is no need to wash the inside of your vagina, even at the vaginal lips as you risk washing the normal flora of the body away leaving the area more exposed to bacteria colonising and therefore an infection developing.

It can also be tempting to want to have a 'quick' bath or wash when your labour has begun and you are about to go into hospital. While a freshen-up may be fine, having a bath or washing your groin area after your waters have broken increases the risks of developing an infection as your birth canal and cervix are open and exposed to the outside world.

Foetal growth

The third trimester is the time when your baby grows at the most rapid rate. In the first trimester the developmental landmarks are happening very quickly and all the organs and systems are being created, but by the third stage, your baby's main focus is to grow in size and lay down fat stores. In fact, your baby is growing at such a rapid rate that he or she will be putting on up to 1/2lb a week so your size is going to change quite a lot during these last 12 weeks.

Milestones in the last trimester

Apart from growing, one of the most important things that occurs in the third trimester is the development and release of lung surfactant which occurs at around the 31 week mark. This means that baby's lungs will be mature enough to cope with life on the outside world with minimal assistance. This does not mean that he or she would not need a day or two in the special care unit, but that the lungs would inflate when born. This is also helped by baby practising breathing by inhaling some of the amniotic fluid over the last few weeks to gently exercise the lungs and muscles involved in the respiratory process.

Another important factor is the skeletal improvements of your baby. He or she will be using up a lot of your calcium stores as their skeleton strengthens and hardens, this means you may need to eat more calcium rich foods to prevent your supplies becoming depleted.

The position of your baby

You will probably find that your baby's movements decrease slightly in the last few weeks as he or she settles into the head down position ready for a normal birth. This can cause your bump to drop quite quickly and while you may not have noticed it yourself, it is likely that others will pass comment on it.

This does not happen for all women of course, as many babies stay in the head up position (breech). If this happens there may be some things you can do to try to help your baby into the head down position. Gentle exercise that opens up the pelvis can encourage a baby to turn and this can be done using yoga, swimming or simply by rocking on all fours for a few minutes every day.

You should also avoid staying in one position for too long, especially sitting, as this will not provide adequate opportunities for your baby to get active and turn itself.

It some cases, your midwife or GP may be able to help turn the baby manually though this is not usually done until very near the due date.

Your body

A pregnant mother's body experiences so many changes during these nine months that it would be difficult to discuss them all. Issues such as heartburn, haemorrhoids, hair growth, varicose veins and leg cramps are all possibilities, but only the most common will be highlighted in this section.

Weight gain

Steady weight gain during most of the third trimester is to be expected and many women find they can put on a stone or more. This can make you feel extremely tired so it is vital that you make sure you rest when you can.

Fortunately, towards the end your weight gain slows while your baby is making his or her final preparations before joining the outside world.

While you may be worried about this rapid weight gain, please do not be tempted to try to diet during this time; much of the weight is made up of amniotic fluid, increased blood volume and the placenta. Weight gain is normal and a healthy part of pregnancy.

Stretch marks

Stretch marks are one of the issues that most women worry about as they can be quite severe and noticeable for many. They occur as the skin struggles to cope with such rapid weight gain and change in body shape.

The good news is that they do fade over time and lose their redness and often aren't too noticeable, but the bad news is that despite using a variety of lotions they aren't really preventable.

There is a general train of thought that suggests you are less likely to get them if your mother didn't have them but really it depends on how quickly and to what size you grow and your skin type.

The only way of minimising (not preventing) them is to use a moisturising cream regularly before you get pregnant so your skin is supple and hydrated and to use products that minimise the look of them. These often contain vitamin E and do not have to be expensive.

In pregnant women, stretch marks normally appear on the abdomen and breasts though they can appear on the hips, legs and arms too.

Breast changes

Changes in your breasts are a sign of a healthy pregnancy and their size and shape can vary from woman to woman. Some women find their breasts hardly change (this does not mean you cannot breastfeed) while others find they grow an enormous amount, change colour and leak breast milk (or colostrum as it is known at this stage).

In the final weeks, your breasts may feel heavy and you may wish to start wearing nursing bras if you are planning to breastfeed. Alternatively, a soft cotton bra that offers support should help alleviate any discomfort from having larger breasts.

Planning for the labour

Preparing for the labour is something that is very personal to each woman or couple, and it should be remembered that even the best laid plans may not come to fruition if you have a baby keen to make an entrance into the world. This does not detract from the importance of making some plans, especially if you think you may have trouble with transport arrangements or contacting your midwife or birthing partner if applicable.

Along with ensuring you have some sort of plan for these concerns, you can prepare yourself by reading plenty of material about labour and childbirth, but remember that often, particularly on the Internet, some stories publicised are those that don't paint the best picture of the experience. You can also help

'Preparing for the labour is something that is very personal to each woman or couple, and it should be remembered that even the best laid plans may not come to fruition if you have a baby keen to make an entrance into the world.'

prepare yourself by attending antenatal classes that help you make decisions, as all the possible options and issues that may arise are likely to be discussed and other couples may have thought of things that you haven't.

Making plans for the labour is also a good way of involving your partner in the birthing process as many of the arrangements can be passed on to them, making it their responsibility to some degree.

Choosing where to have your baby

Deciding on where to have the baby may be a decision that comes easily to you, while for others careful consideration of all the benefits and disadvantages may help.

Do not think that just because you are an older parent that you must have your baby in hospital as you may be able to have a home birth providing there have been no complications during the pregnancy. This is an issue you must discuss at length with your midwife and you must both agree that you are a suitable candidate for a home birth.

Your options of where to have your baby may include your local hospital, a midwife led birthing centre or at home. In order to make the most informed decision it is useful to arm yourself with all the facts before making a definite choice.

Who will be with you?

Most women who are in a stable relationship will choose their partner to accompany them throughout the birth and will involve them in the birthing process. Others who do not have a partner, or who's partner works away, may have to decide if they would like someone else to experience the birth of their child with them.

If the woman's partner is not the selected birthing partner the next most obvious choice is a close family member or friend. This person should be someone who you feel totally at ease with and not self-conscious, someone who you trust and someone who will be able to offer you the support you need during the labour and birth. It is also important to choose someone who will be able to accompany you at any time during the day; it isn't very beneficial to choose someone who has a lot of commitments elsewhere and who won't be available at two o'clock in the morning.

Preparing for the birth

You may or may not have been thinking too much about the actual birth up until now, but suddenly you find your due date is just around the corner and the prospect of actually giving birth can be quite daunting, or perhaps an exciting adventure.

Making plans for the birth not only helps you but also helps your midwife try to make the experience as comfortable and pleasant for you as possible.

Most midwives encourage the use of birth plans to try to aid this time but do remember that it may not always go according to plan. Where possible, your healthcare team will try to facilitate your requests.

What is a birth plan?

A birth plan is a written proposal that includes all of your ideas and plans that you would like during the actual childbirth. This includes the types of pain relief you would like, where and how you are hoping to have your baby, the people you want with you and what you don't really want.

Where possible try to word it politely and carefully and instead of making it a list of commands, make it a general document that explains your reasons for your requests. It may be helpful to sit down with your birthing partner or midwife while you are writing your birth plan as there may be ideas you would like to include that you haven't thought of yourself.

Again, it is important to reiterate that this is just a plan, and in some circumstances your ideas might have to be overruled for health and safety reasons.

'You may or may not have been thinking too much about the actual birth up until now, but suddenly you find your due date is just around the corner and the prospect of actually giving birth can be quite daunting, or perhaps an exciting adventure.'

Changing your mind about your birth plan

Your birth plan is your own private document and you can change your wishes at any time and it is helpful if you write down your new ideas, possibly with a short explanation of why you feel the need to change your mind.

Of course if you have written in your birth plan that you want to have your baby with no pain relief and find that during the labour you do wish to have something, your midwife will understand and be flexible about your birth plan.

'Of course if you have written in your birth plan that you want to have your baby with no pain relief and find that during the labour you do wish to have something, your midwife will understand and be flexible about your birth plan.'

Packing your bag

Knowing what to pack in your hospital or birthing bag is sometimes a fairly big issue for women and many find that once they have packed their bag, they check it many times in case they have forgotten something.

Your midwife will probably be able to offer some guidance on the subject but there are some essential items that you really should include.

- Your maternity folder or notes.
- Your birth plan.
- Clothes for your baby.
- Nappies.
- A baby blanket.
- Sanitary towels (not tampons).
- Clothes for going home in (often maternity clothes will continue to be needed for a few days or even weeks after the birth).
- Slippers, socks, night clothes.
- Toiletries.
- Hairbrush and bands if you have long hair.
- Your favourite snacks or drinks.
- Your own pillow.
- Magazines or a book.

- A few old pairs of underwear (or disposable ones).
- A car seat if you are travelling by car (with instructions).
- A going home outfit for baby.
- Hat and mittens if it is cold.

You may also want to include some photos, a camera and some personal effects, particularly if you want to use something from home as your focal point.

Other useful tips

There are several things you can do to make the experience as painless and comfortable as it can be and don't be afraid to try them.

For example, it can be very helpful to make noise during labour and will provide you with an enormous amount of relief so don't be shy and grin and bear the pain; vocalising actually does make the pain seem less severe.

If it helps, rock back and forth or use a rocking chair or beanbag to find a more comfortable position as the movement will help both you and your baby through the contractions.

Being anxious is normal but try not to be so terrified of labour that you make yourself feel unwell. There are many pain relieving options available and women have been giving birth for many hundreds of years, often in the most extreme circumstances.

If you are feeling so scared that you dread the labour, please speak to your midwife or GP for further advice on how you can relax more when the time comes.

When labour finally does kick in, try not to be in too much of a hurry to get to hospital, especially if your pain levels aren't excruciating, as this can be a costly exercise. In many cases, the cervix takes a long time to dilate enough to deliver a baby and staying at home not only is more relaxing for you, but you may find that you are sent home from hospital and told to come back later on.

'There are several things you can do to make the experience as painless and comfortable as it can be and don't be afraid to try them.'

Pain relief

The subject of pain relief is often a very big issue for pregnant women as some people want as much as they can have, others want to try to have no pain relief and some are just happy to see how they cope without having a definite plan.

It is always very helpful to have a general understanding of the types of pain relief on offer so you can make an informed decision about what type of support and pain relief you may want to try.

TENS

The term TENS stands for Transcutaneous Electrical Nerve Stimulation and is a good way of receiving pain relief without taking any medications.

It is a small machine that comes with sticky pads that are placed in strategic places during labour and delivers electrical impulses through the skin which alters how the body reacts to pain stimulation. It works by encouraging the release of endorphins in the body, which are nature's own pain relieving chemicals that alter the degree of pain we experience.

Along with the unit is a small hand-piece that can allow the user to control how strong delivered impulses are going to be. It is recommended that the TENS machine should be used for at least 40 minutes before it starts having its maximum effect and that low grade impulses are used between contractions and a higher strength is used when a contraction starts. It carries no risk to either mother or baby and will not leave you with any nasty side effects.

If you would like to try a TENS machine, please do let your midwife know well in advance as a machine will need booking for your use.

Entonox

Otherwise known as gas and air, entonox is a very commonly used substance during labour and childbirth. It is made up of half oxygen and half nitrous oxide, carries no odour or colour and is a very good way of managing pain during labour.

It has the additional advantage of being portable which means it can be used in any birthing setting providing your midwife has some on board.

Another great advantage of using entonox is that is can be controlled by the user and can be delivered via a face mask or through a mouthpiece that is placed between the teeth. Deep breaths are taken and inhaled and the resulting effect should be quite calming, taking the edge off the pain. Being able to control the delivery of the gas, especially through a mouthpiece, also offers a welcome distraction during each contraction.

Entonox leaves the system very quickly but sometimes makes the person feel dizzy and slightly nauseous though this also passes very rapidly.

Pain relieving injections

Having an injection during labour used to be a very common way of receiving pain relief but experts have found the advantages may not be as good as first thought.

The most frequently used drug is called pethidine which is given as an injection to the buttock. It takes around 20-30 minutes to start working to full effect and may last several hours. Rather than actually lessening the pain it more often works by relaxing the mother so that she deals with the pain in a more productive way.

The down side to using pethidine is that it does affect the baby and may mean that the baby needs some oxygen when first born or that he or she is quite drowsy for the first few days, which may hinder the instigation of a good breastfeeding regime.

Massage

Believe it or not, massage actually offers a great way of relieving pain and is also a very good way of involving your partner in the birthing process.

Massage works by promoting the release of endorphins which lessen the pain experienced and can even block the pain signals to the brain. It also has the added bonuses of keeping you relaxed, offers a distraction and can be performed anywhere.

'Believe it or not, massage actually offers a great way of relieving pain and is also a very good way of involving your partner in the birthing process.'

If you want to use massage oils, it is advised that you consult with an aromatherapist as some of the oils available are not safe for pregnant women and may have a negative effect on both you and the baby.

To get the most out of massage during labour, it is recommended that you pick up a good book on the subject and do some background reading on the best massage techniques for tackling labour pains. Your GP or midwife may be able to recommend a title or try a visit to your local library.

Epidurals

The use of epidurals continues to be a very popular choice among labouring women. It works by delivering a pain relief down a tube to your spinal area. This must be administered by an anaesthetist so is therefore not available for home births or in midwife led units.

After the drugs have been administered, the whole pelvic area becomes increasingly numb until often no pain can be felt.

The negative side of having an epidural is that it does tend to make the second stage of labour slightly longer and may increase the chances of needing assistance during the actual delivery (something which older mothers are already at risk from anyway).

It is wise to consider whether you want to receive an epidural in advance of your labour as it may mean you have to change your plans for where you want to have your baby and often this has further implications such as travelling to and from hospital, car park costs and actually learning the best way to the hospital.

Choosing to have no pain relief

Some women elect to try to have no pain relief during the labour and want to experience every part of it without any side effects. This is absolutely fine but it is always best to have a back-up just in case the pain overwhelms you.

If are going to try to have no pain relief, there are some natural remedies that may help you pass the pain during each contraction. Music offers a good medium for allowing your emotions to come through and some women like classical for its crescendos whereas others like the fast pace of dance music and some even like to try to listen to something calming and peaceful to help them remain calm throughout the delivery. The choice is very individual and each person will have their own taste and expectation of how they think they will manage the pain.

Another good distraction is to have a focal point during the labour. This can be anything from a personal item such as a photo album, a religious effect such as a crucifix or your birthing partner. Again this offers a very good distraction and something to concentrate on during the apex of each contraction but you must make sure that the item you are going to use is packed into your bag so you don't forget it.

Summing Up

The third trimester is an exciting if somewhat nerve-racking time for pregnant women and their partners. The baby is due very soon and the arrangements for the labour, birth and beyond have to be made during this time.

Also during these weeks you will find your body changes significantly, you are often more tired and your partner becomes a little more protective of you as the delivery becomes more imminent.

By making plans and knowing all the facts regarding the labour, birth and pain relief, you will be more equipped to cope with whatever experiences you are about to undergo.

While it can be a time for anxiety, it is also a good time to savour the last few weeks of being able to enjoy your baby on your own before everyone else gets to meet him or her, so enjoy as much of it as you can.

Chapter Nine

The Labour and Delivery

All of a sudden your due date is approaching and you are probably beginning to feel a little anxious at what is about to happen to you, how you'll cope and whether everything will go smoothly. These emotions are normal and if you weren't feeling a little worried people would probably think you were a tiny bit odd!

Hopefully by understanding every stage of the last part of your pregnancy you will feel more confident that you will cope just fine and begin to look forward to the birth and meeting your new baby. After all, if it was that bad, would women continue to have more children in the future?

The early signs of labour

For some women, especially those having their first baby, recognising the early signs of labour is not as obvious as they thought it would be. True labour often begins in the back and then spreads round to the entire abdomen and may feel like strong Braxton Hicks at first.

For others, the waters breaking may be the first sign, and although it can suddenly gush, it is not uncommon for it to happen as a slow trickle, often being mistaken as urinary incontinence if it is very slow.

It is helpful to know the most common signs so that you are given a little indication of whether you are experiencing true labour, or simply having a bit of practice before the big event.

'Hopefully by understanding every stage of the last part of your pregnancy you will feel more confident that you will cope just fine and begin to look forward to the birth and meeting your new baby.'

False labour

False labour is a term given when women believe they are in labour when in fact they aren't.

Often this is a result of the Braxton Hicks contractions becoming more frequent and stronger, sometimes with a regular pattern to them. This can be very misleading for women (and send their partners into a panic) and even those who have had babies in the past can be fooled when this happens.

Sometimes a false labour can last several hours before the pains subside, often leaving the woman pain free for another few weeks.

Recognising false labour is difficult but, on the whole, the pains tend to start like period pains and stay around the lower pelvis and lower back and can sometimes be eased by changing position. In true labour the pain can consume your whole abdomen, your back and gets worse as time passes.

What is a 'show'?

Some women, though not all, will experience a 'show' in the days or even weeks before the labour and often this is a sign that labour is imminent.

A show occurs when the mucous plug that sits at the cervix comes away. It is a thick, sticky, jelly-like plug that may or may not have a blood stained appearance.

If you are unaware that a show could happen it can be quite alarming, but please feel reassured that it is perfectly fine to lose this plug and no harm will come to you or your baby. It is simply nature's way of telling the cervix that it will be due to start opening soon.

Niggles and twinges

You may have found that throughout the last few weeks of your pregnancy you have felt more niggles and twinges than before and find that you are asking yourself 'is this it?' time after time. This is normal and most women suffer from niggling pains from time to time. Practice contractions do become stronger and more regular, often feeling like labour has begun, only for you to find that two hours later the pains have stopped.

If at any point you are feeling niggly pains and you believe your waters have broken, you are bleeding or your baby stops moving, please see a midwife who can check if everything is okay.

The first stage of labour

Labour is divided into three stages: the start of the contractions and your cervix dilating being the first, the delivery of the baby being the second and the final stage is the delivery of the placenta.

The good news is that although the chances of needing a caesarean are higher in older women, there are no real differences in the labour whether you are young or more mature.

Contractions

A contraction is the involuntary tightening of the womb (uterine muscle) which is the largest muscle in a female body when it is carrying a baby to term.

The start of the contraction is controlled by a release of hormones that can occur at any time, leaving labour almost out of our control.

As the top of the womb tightens against the baby, the lower half stretches and opens allowing the baby to descend lower into the pelvis.

If you believe you are in labour, try timing the contractions by starting to count in seconds from the start of one contraction to the very end and then starting again for the duration of the rest period. This shows the duration of a contraction and how long there is between each one.

Dilation of the cervix

The cervix is a remarkable organ capable of great changes both good and bad. During labour the cervix actually thins out and opens up to let the babies pass through to the vagina. This is no mean feat when normally it is closed very tightly and has to open to a full 10 centimetres, all without you even knowing.

Your midwife will check intermittently how far your cervix has opened to try to gauge how far into your labour you are and when baby will be ready to meet you.

How long do I stay at home for?

Most midwives suggest that providing you are managing the pain and your membranes are intact that you wait until the contractions are around five minutes apart and have been for about an hour before venturing to the hospital.

This is of course only a guide and your body will probably let you know when the time is right to make your way over or contact a midwife for advice.

It is at this stage that you will be glad of having pre-packed a bag, prepared all relevant phone numbers and know exactly how to get to the hospital or birthing unit.

When you arrive at the delivery suite, you will have your blood pressure and pulse monitored, be attached to a foetal monitor to check the progress of the baby and also be examined to see how far your cervix is dilated. These tests will help notify your midwife of any problems and will also help determine roughly how long before the baby is due to enter the birth canal.

Rupture of membranes (waters breaking)

Yet another dread of expectant mums is wondering when the waters will break – again, this is unfortunately not something you can control. The membranes may suddenly 'go' in the middle of the supermarket, but much more likely, they will break gently and leave you with a persistent trickle rather than a huge gush.

For some, the membranes have to be broken by the midwife and this involves the use of something similar to a crochet hook that while not being painful or harmful to the baby, can be a little uncomfortable.

Keeping mobile

One of the most advantageous things you can do in the early stages of labour is to keep on the move. Not only will this keep your labour shorter, it will encourage your baby to move down and help you to cope with the contractions. It also offers a distraction and helps pass what can be a very long time. Lots of labouring women find it helpful to have their partner periodically rub their lower back or provide massage during this time.

The second stage of labour

The second stage of labour is when you get to first meet your new baby. It begins when your cervix is fully dilated to 10 cm allowing your baby to pass through and ends when your baby enters the world.

During this time your midwife will guide you through the process, telling when and how to push. This stage can be very hard work and will require even more energy than the previous stage, even for those of you who may spend several hours having regular contractions.

'One of the most advantageous things you can do in the early stages of labour is to keep on the move. Not only will this keep your labour shorter, it will encourage your baby to move down and help you to cope with the contractions.'

What is the second stage of labour?

As your cervix dilates to its maximum size, your baby will descend down and its head will rest at the top of the birth canal ready for you to help push it through. The baby may descend down very quickly, or may take a little while. However, both you and your midwife will know when the time to start pushing arrives as you will feel a strong sensation to bear down.

With each contraction your baby will go lower and lower into the pelvis. Sometimes your midwife may be able to help you move things along if this is not happening, or you may prefer to wait until nature allows this to happen naturally.

Due to the size and shape of the baby's head and your anatomy, the head will advance and then recede slightly with each push, and this can go on for some time.

When the top of the head has reached the cervix and is starting to make its way through (this is called crowning), you may be asked, or if not ask your midwife, if you would like to feel the head. Often you can feel lots of hair or may even want to use a mirror to see what is going on and to catch that first glimpse of your child.

'For some women a few pushes is all that is needed to pass the head, shortly followed by the rest of the baby, while others may find themselves in this stage for hours.'

How long does it last?

There is no easy answer to this question as each labour is very different. The strength of each contraction, the position you are in, the energy you put into each push and the work being done by your abdominal muscles will contribute to the second stage of labour and a time frame cannot be estimated.

For some women, a few pushes is all that is needed to pass the head, shortly followed by the rest of the baby, while others may find themselves in this stage for hours.

During the pushing stage, your midwife may tell you to stop pushing intermittently. This is because the skin and tissues between your vagina and your anus can tear quite easily and by controlled pushing, the area will be encouraged to stretch more slowly and therefore accommodate the size of the baby rather than being forced to an unnatural stretch and tear.

You may also be told that you need an episiotomy to help deliver the baby. This requires the injection of a local anaesthetic to the area to numb it before it is cut. While the anaesthetic might sting for a few seconds, many women tend not to feel this too much as the pain from the contractions and pushing is stronger.

Tips for coping

Coping with the second stage of labour can be handled in a few different ways. Listening to the guidance of your midwife and birthing partner and focusing on what they are saying can be a good way of staying in control. For others, vocalising the pain can be a therapeutic way of managing the pain, but above all else, remember that you are about to meet your child for the very first time and this is indeed one of life's most special moments.

The last push!

The last push is most likely to give you the greatest sense of relief and achievement. When the head has been delivered, it is not so much effort to push the rest of the baby out.

As soon as the head has been delivered, your midwife will quickly check the airway to make sure it is not obstructed (this is because the baby has been subjected to a lot of fluid and other substances) and will provide a little suction to the nose and mouth if needed. They will also check that the baby's umbilical cord is not wrapped around the neck as this can sometimes happen and is easily resolved by unwrapping it by hand.

It is not uncommon for women to worry when they do not hear the baby cry straightaway, but not all babies are born screaming and if the room is warm and quiet, he or she may be content enough for the time being.

If you are hoping to have skin to skin contact, you may want to either raise or remove your top at this stage so the midwife can place your baby to your chest as soon as the rest has been delivered; you do not have to wait for the cord to be cut to have skin to skin contact.

'The last push is most likely to give you the greatest sense of relief and achievement. When the head has been delivered, it is not so much effort to push the rest of the baby out.'

The third stage of labour

The third stage of labour is something that not all expectant mothers are familiar with. The birthing process does not end when the baby has been delivered as the placenta and membranes have to be evacuated from the womb too.

This stage of labour can occur naturally taking slightly longer or can be medically managed by the administration of a medicine that is injected into your thigh after birth and encourages the womb to contract until the products are expelled.

What is the third stage of labour?

The relief you will feel after giving birth to your baby is something almost indescribable and the fact that it is not quite over yet probably won't be the first thought in your mind. The delivery of the placenta is important though and hopefully, for most women, it will come away easily and in one piece.

The membranes are the sac that contained the fluid that surrounded the baby. Within this is the placenta which is often larger than most people had imagined. As the membranes no longer contain fluid they, along with the placenta, look a little like a deflated balloon. If you are a smoker however, your placenta may come away in pieces and take longer to deliver, occasionally needing the assistance of medical staff.

What happens to the placenta?

Immediately after the placenta has been expelled by the body, it will be checked by the midwife to make sure it is complete and there are no components left inside the womb. After this it will either be disposed of at the hospital (sent for incineration) or sent for tests if needed.

If for some reason you explicitly want to take the placenta home, you must mention this in your birth plan and the hospital will be able to tell you their local policy on this matter.

Speeding up the third stage

You will probably be asked at some stage during the labour whether you want to receive the injection to speed up the third stage of labour. The injection is given into the thigh as the baby enters the world. Due to the strength of the contraction and the effort you are putting into pushing, you will probably be unaware of the injection and feel no discomfort. Also, it is surprising for women to find out that delivering the placenta is in no way as hard as delivering the baby and it is often not something that is particularly remembered about the birth.

Methods of delivery

Babies can be born in a number of ways with varying degrees of assistance from medical staff.

You may or may not have planned to have some form of intervention during the birth, but many births do often require the use of intervention as a matter of urgency or if things are not progressing as planned.

As older mothers have been found to be more likely to require assistance, it is probably going to be helpful if you understand all the different terms and methods that may be a possibility when you are due to give birth.

Normal vaginal delivery

A normal vaginal delivery is the term used to describe someone who has given birth with minimal assistance, with the baby proceeding down the vaginal canal in the natural manner and being born this way.

It may or may not be accompanied by the use of an episiotomy, and is otherwise known as a natural birth.

'Science has shown that water births can have a very good impact on blood pressure and lessen the severity of labour pains.'

Ventouse/vacuum delivery

A ventouse delivery involves placing a suction cup on the baby's head and the application of a vacuum through the cup which is attached to a machine. It is generally tried before a forceps delivery as there is less risk of trauma to the vulva and pelvic floor.

The cup is applied to the baby's head so that it fits quite snugly. It is generally not dangerous or uncomfortable for either mother or baby but the machine can be quite noisy so don't be alarmed.

Forceps delivery

Nobody really wants to have their baby delivered by forceps, but on many occasions the use of the instrument can be life saving.

The forceps are large, spoon shaped instruments that fit around the sides of the baby's head as he or she is being delivered. Often the baby is stuck or becoming distressed and your GP and midwife have decided that assistance is needed to ensure the baby is born safely, but this will depend on where and how your baby is laying in the birth canal.

Occasionally the forceps can leave indentations or bruises on the baby's head or face and, although this can be distressing for the parents, the marks will fade quite quickly leaving no long term effects.

If a forceps delivery fails and a ventouse has already been tried, you may need to undergo a caesarean section.

Caesarean section

There are a number of reasons why a caesarean section may be needed to deliver your baby, either for your health and safety or that of your baby.

The procedure is a surgical operation that involves making a low abdominal incision and opening the womb itself to deliver the baby and the placenta. The wound is closed in layers and most surgeons can leave you with a minimal scar that cannot be seen very easily. The procedure can be carried out using a top up to your existing epidural, a spinal anaesthetic or a general anaesthetic if needed.

Unless you have previously discussed the option of a caesarean with your GP or midwife, the decision to proceed with one often occurs during labour when things aren't progressing as hoped, your baby is at risk or your own safety is becoming compromised.

You may have been in labour for some time and have a lot of pain relief on board when the subject is approached by staff, but you will still be asked for your consent to the procedure unless it is a life or death situation.

Water births

Water births continue to be very popular and can be offered in many hospitals, midwife led units and even at home in some areas. There is some very reassuring scientific evidence that supports the use of water births as it has many benefits for both baby and mother.

For the mother, the feeling of being in warm water can be very comforting and means they feel lighter and therefore have less physical pressure on their body. It can also be a good way of relieving back ache, allowing the mother to feel free and also aids relaxation especially if combined with music, soft lighting and scented oils.

Science has shown that water births can have a very good impact on blood pressure and lessen the severity of labour pains.

In the past there were concerns about the safety of water births, but experts now agree that providing the water is the right depth and temperature and baby is brought to the surface in the correct way, there are few risks and the benefits generally outweigh the risks.

Older mothers and home births

Before midwifery was developed as a profession, and when hospitals were built to care solely for the very sick, women traditionally gave birth at home either with the assistance of a relative or friend.

Nowadays having a home birth seems to be less favourable among women as they fear something will go wrong and there will be no medical provisions for assistance.

Older mothers in particular are all too aware that they are more at risk of needing intervention during labour or delivery, but this shouldn't stop you considering the option of a home birth if you really want one.

Is it safe to have a home birth?

In effect, anyone can have a home birth, especially if they are in active labour and the baby decides to come very quickly!

The government is trying to find ways of giving women more choice about where they give birth including at home, but in some areas it may still not be a recommended practice and if you really do want a home birth, you may have to pursue your request with some vigour.

The research on the subject of older mothers and the risks of having a home birth is quite vague. Although it does seem they are more at risk of requiring medical intervention, the reasons for this are not clear cut and many professionals agree that the expectations of the mothers and the attitudes of healthcare staff also have significant roles to play in the increase of intervention.

To arrange a home birth, please speak to your midwife. If he or she is not supportive try your GP or the person in charge of your community midwives' office.

Am I too old to have a home birth?

As you will have been observed closely throughout your pregnancy, it is hoped that any complications will have been detected by the time delivery arrives. Due to this your GP and midwife will have a good idea whether you are a suitable candidate for a home birth or not. If you have any conditions that increase your risks of complications it is probably in your best interests to have your baby in hospital or at least a midwife led unit where there is more back-up should you need it.

The benefits of home births

One of the biggest benefits of having a home birth is that you are more in control of what is going on. You are in your comfortable area and can come and go as you please within your own surroundings. You can choose to deliver anywhere in your home (as long as your midwife has reasonable access) and may decide to go from chair to chair until you are comfortable.

You will also have the luxury of being able to watch a film, listen to a CD or even use the phone in between contractions if you wish. There isn't the added stress of having to make your way to the hospital and the maternity unit and you won't need to pack a bag to take with you. If you wish to, have some snacks or special drinks during labour, you have your own stocked fridge with all your favourite treats inside.

Finally, your baby will be born into his or her home environment and will not be exposed to the hospital surroundings that may be too hot, too cold and at home will even be more protected against infections.

The disadvantages of home births

Having a home birth doesn't go without some disadvantages, however, and these need some consideration before a final decision is made.

You home will not have the types of monitoring offered in hospital which check on the progress of both you and your baby and serve as an early warning system if something is not going as planned.

There is also the risk of needing some assistance with the delivery which is not available in your own home and you may lose precious minutes going to the hospital.

Also, there is the consideration of who is going to tidy the mess after the delivery. Although you can use many waterproof mats and sheets (that your midwife may provide, possibly at a small fee), it cannot be guaranteed that all the fluids will be contained on these.

Summing Up

Despite all the plans you may have had for your labour and delivery, you may find that your experience will be totally different than you had expected. Hopefully by making yourself more aware of what may happen or by knowing all of the options available to you, you will feel more in control of your situation and your expectations will be more realistic.

Putting some thought into the benefits and disadvantages of all the options available to you will help both you and the medical team make the best choices for you and baby.

Chapter Ten

You and Your Baby

Bonding with your baby

Bonding with your new baby is very important and can be achieved whether you are allowed to take them home straightaway or if they need a little help in the first days or weeks in the special care unit.

Your voice will bring lots of comfort to your baby as he or she will have grown used to it over the last nine months. Meaningful touch is also very important and providing you follow the guidelines within the special care baby unit, there is little reason why you shouldn't be permitted to touch your baby.

If you are lucky enough to be able to take your newborn straight home, then spend the first few days getting to know each other on a level that only a parent can understand.

Lots of mums and dads know their baby's scent and gradually learn every line on their fingers and every detail of their face and this can be so easily achieved by allowing yourself quiet time to just study each other. Your baby will enjoy the closeness of feeling you so near and will probably learn to settle by the sound of your voice and touch of your skin.

Why bonding is important

Experts have found that bonding is an essential part of raising a child and that it is very beneficial to the health and welfare of the child. It is not something that occurs immediately for everyone and often takes time and effort to achieve, but there are ways of encouraging the bonding process.

'Bonding with your new baby is very important and can be achieved whether you are allowed to take them home straightaway or if they need a little help in the first days or weeks in the special care unit.'

Skin to skin contact

Skin to skin contact is something that is now widely advocated among midwives. Expert studies have found that placing the naked newborn straight onto the mother's bare skin immediately after birth has huge benefits to successful breastfeeding and also for the developing relationship and interfacing between mother and child. This interaction can be positively seen many years later showing that those first few minutes of intimacy make a huge difference to the long term relationship of mother and child.

Communicating with your baby

Communicating with your baby from birth is absolutely essential to bonding with baby and establishing a mother/child relationship.

It has been heard from some new mothers that there is no point in talking to a new baby as they don't understand you or respond, but actually this is not true at all.

Your baby's brain will be full of activity from the moment he or she is born and will want to develop at a very rapid rate. Communication skills are one of the single most important life skills you can give to your child and by encouraging your baby to listen, make sense of your voice and communicate through touch and eye contact, you will be giving them a very precious gift.

Babies are on the whole fairly sociable and will enjoy interacting with you when they are awake. It also provides a reassuring way of building up trust and understanding between both of you.

Bonding with dad

The early days of parenting can be quite tough for new fathers as the new mum can be highly protective of their baby and want to do everything themselves. But equally the new dad is just getting to know his baby from scratch when the mum has slowly been getting to know the little one over the past few months.

This does not mean that dads don't bond as much with the baby, but it may mean they have to work a little harder at establishing the relationship.

The best ways for the dad to get involved are to try to take part in everyday routines such as bathing, dressing or feeding the baby. This also gives mum some rest time and the baby will slowly learn that these times are for a one-to-one session with dad and will look forward to spending this time with him each day.

Breast or bottle?

A number of mums-to-be know straightaway whether they are going to breastfeed or not and some feel very strongly about this. The advantages of breastfeeding are widely publicised and far outweigh the benefits of bottle feeding. However, not all women can breastfeed successfully, though half the battle seems to be the attitudes towards breastfeeding and the mother's perseverance.

It can be beneficial to decide whether you are going to breastfeed or not before the baby is born, but equally it may be that you are going to decide immediately after the delivery when you first have skin to skin contact. This is a good way of letting your baby decide, as many newborns automatically head for the nipple when laid on mum's bare chest.

If you wish to breastfeed, your midwife or other staff member will guide you through initiating the process, and can inform you of any breastfeeding support groups in your area that you may like to attend when you take yourbaby home.

Advantages of breastfeeding

There are many benefits to breastfeeding and these can be good for both mother and child.

Breast milk contains exactly the right balance of components to satisfy a baby and provide all the nutrients he or she needs. Breastfed babies seem to settle more easily and have fewer childhood ear infections and episodes of vomiting and diarrhoea. Experts are also continuing with research that may prove childhood obesity is less likely to occur in breastfed babies also. There are also studies that show the incidence of asthma, eczema and diabetes is lower in those who were breastfed as a baby, and that these children tend to perform better emotionally and intellectually.

On the whole, breastfed babies also seem to suffer less with colic and do not have as much wind to bring up as bottle fed babies, possibly because the sucking action on the breast does not let any air enter the digestive tract.

It isn't just the baby who benefits from breastfeeding as there are an equal number of benefits for the mum too. One of the most important issues is women who breastfeed stand a much lower chance of developing breast cancer in later life and will also be more protected against other serious illnesses such as ovarian cancer, Type 2 diabetes and may well be less likely to suffer from postnatal depression.

If these facts are not enough to persuade you to try breastfeeding, then maybe the financial gain will: breastfeeding is free and you won't have to spend money on a steriliser, formula and bottles unless you are going to express the milk.

It may also be easier to cope with night feeds as you can simply jump out of bed, feed and wind your baby and then settle back to sleep, rather than having to make a bottle up, warm it and then rinse it out before re-sterilising (not a nice prospect in the middle of the night).

'On the whole, breastfed babies also seem to suffer less with colic and do not have as much wind to bring up as bottle fed babies, possibly because the sucking action on the breast does not let any air enter the digestive tract.'

Advantages of bottle feeding

The number of benefits of bottle feeding is in no way as exceptional as those of breastfeeding.

The main advantages are not health benefits, merely convenience.

- Bottle feeding is a good way of sharing the responsibility of raising a baby as the dad or another family member can take over when you are tired, especially during the night.

- It seems that bottle fed babies tend to need to be fed less often as the formula is harder to digest so keeps baby fuller for longer. Also, you can see exactly how much milk baby is taking at each feed and can increase or decrease as you need to.

- Many women who have to return to work very soon after having their baby find that bottle feeding is the best option as finding a regime when you work (particularly shift work or fulltime) is very difficult to achieve.

What do I need to bottle feed?

If you want to bottle feed, there are a number of things you need to organise before your baby is born as bringing your baby home from hospital with no provision for making feeds is asking for trouble.

To start with you need to decide what type of sterilising unit you need. All the baby's bottles, bottle rings, teats, dummies and teethers should be sterilised for at least the first year, making sure that all deposits of milk are thoroughly removed from the feeding equipment as this can cause a lot of tummy upsets.

The main methods of sterilising are boiling, microwaving, steaming and cold water sterilising using a chemical product. There are various pros and cons to each method of sterilising and a little research into the various types may be useful before you make a purchase.

You will also need some bottles (about six), making sure the teats are slow-flow for newborns and fit into your steriliser. Also needed is a bottle brush that can reach easily into the bottom of the bottle without scratching the plastic or splitting the teat.

How do I choose which formula to feed my baby?

Choosing your formula is a decision you can usually make with your midwife.

It may be that you choose a product because of its reputation, its price, because your friends or family have used it in the past or simply because your maternity unit stocks it and offers it to you when your baby has his or her first feed.

You may have very particular ideas about which formula to use so it is important to discuss these issues with your midwife in case any special provisions have to be made when your baby is born.

Bathing and changing your baby

Many women think that bathing a baby is easy and something that comes naturally, while others may need a lesson in baby-bathing. It really is in your best interests to learn the correct way to bathe your baby even if you feel it is easy, as it may help avoid an unnecessary accident.

Bathing your baby is a fantastic way of bonding with your baby as both parties usually enjoy the experience. It is also a brilliant way of involving your partner or family in looking after the baby and giving you a few minutes peace and quiet.

How often does a baby need bathing?

Newborn babies are usually either asleep, laying quietly or being held so they don't become dirty very easily, so unless your baby really enjoys having a bath, it isn't necessary to bath him or her every day.

They do, however, sweat quite a lot and can do little to stop the sweat collecting on their skin so a bath every other day is perfectly acceptable.

How to bathe a baby

Your midwife or another healthcare professional in the hospital will be happy to show you the correct way to bathe a baby while protecting your back from feeling the strain of bending over for too long.

In general, the guidelines are to make sure the room is warm enough for baby to be comfortable in without clothing, the water warm but not hot (test by dipping in your elbow), cleansing agents should be free from perfumes and colours and be a make that has been specially created for babies, and the water shouldn't be too deep (about five to six inches).

Get everything ready, including the towel and nappy for after the bath and have it handy. Strip your baby down to the nappy and wrap in a towel. Using a soft cotton wash-cloth or cotton wool, gently wipe over the baby's face using the bath water with no soap, making sure you get behind their ears but not in the eyes or mouth. When you have finished, remove the nappy and place one arm around the baby's back allowing your hand to grip firmly but not too hard under the baby's arm. Allow the baby to rest back on your forearm and wrist for the bath. Gently lower him or her into the water and use your free hand to gently wash your baby making sure soap is used sparingly and is rinsed thoroughly.

Bathing products for newborns

For baby's first few baths, it really isn't necessary to use anything except plain, warm water as the chemicals in many of the products will be drying to the skin.

It is also not too important to go overboard with talcum powder as, again, this can be very drying. More important is to make sure that all areas of the baby are clean and dried properly so soreness can be prevented.

Cleaning around the umbilical cord

It may not perhaps look very pleasant but the umbilical cord stump is what connected you to your baby for the entire pregnancy and so is very important.

When the cord has been clamped and cut, it receives no blood supply so eventually it will die and fall off; often a thought that makes people feel a little queasy!

The area does, however, need some care and attention to prevent it getting sore or infected while you wait for it to fall off. Gently cleansing around the area in the morning and before bed should be sufficient to keep it clean.

Sometimes the cord stumps do get a little pus collection which is relatively normal, but if the pus develops and bleeding, redness and pain occur, please speak to your midwife as it may be infected and need treatment.

Getting enough sleep

The subject of sleep is one of the most frequently heard issues that affect new parents and unfortunately there is no easy remedy for getting more sleep.

Your baby may cry, be unsettled, have trapped wind, need feeding very frequently or may just find it takes a while to establish a routine, causing you to lose several hours sleep a night.

The good news is that newborns often sleep during the day so you can use this time to catch up on a few hours too. If this is your first baby, it is easier than if you have other children or commitments that prevent you sleeping during the day.

If you are really exhausted, why not ask a friend or relative to take your baby out for a few hours once or twice a week so that you can have a peaceful lay down?

'If you are really exhausted, why not ask a friend or relative to take baby out for a few hours once or twice a week so that you can have a peaceful lay down?'

You may worry that your household chores are not getting done to the standard you would like, but do remember that you have the rest of your life to do housework and that your baby is only this little for a few months, so try not to worry too much about housework.

Creating a quiet and relaxed environment

If necessary, put a sign up at the front door that says 'do not disturb – baby sleeping' and unplug the phone. Most people will understand and not trouble you, giving you the time and space to rest with your baby or settle a tense baby.

Also try creating a very softly lit room with just enough light to be comfortable without feeling intimidated by the dark. Your baby may want to watch you when you sleep, feeling reassured that you are still there without crying for you if you can't be seen.

Consequences of not getting enough sleep

It is very valuable to not underestimate the worthiness of sleep as you will soon feel the consequences if you are getting not your quota. Most new parents will feel sleep deprived and cope quite well, but some very difficult babies can push you to the limits of your tolerance and ability to function normally.

Essentially, with a newborn you must sleep when you can even if this is at strange times during the day; you will reap the benefits later.

Don't worry about sleeping during the day, it doesn't last forever as most babies find a sleep/wake routine quite quickly, as long as they do not have trapped wind or colic and are satisfied and comfortable.

Asking for support

Having a baby is hard work, what with tiredness, unpredictable feeding times, crying, emotional upheaval and learning to share your time and surroundings with a baby so it is no surprise that it can get a little overwhelming at times. We all need support and there aren't many women who can go it alone without feeling a little weighed down by the experience.

There is no failure in needing to ask for support from those around you, and even things like letting someone make you a meal, clean the floors or even sending your ironing out to be done for a few months can really ease the pressure.

If, however, you feel you need more help, there are many places you can go to seek advice on the matter, many of which are confidential.

To begin with though, most of the time seeking support from family and friends is enough to help you get through the tough times and many of these people will be thrilled to help you.

Knowing when you need help

Despite our best intentions and planning, sometimes our hormones or even extreme tiredness can catch up with us and make us miserable or feel unable to cope. Far from being a weakness, identifying when you need a little help is actually a strength and something we all have to do from time to time. Maybe you just need to hand over some of the jobs or responsibility of looking after the baby to your partner while you rest or perhaps a friend or relative could help you out.

If, however, you feel you need additional help and are struggling to cope with even the most basic of everyday tasks, please do speak to your GP or midwife as soon as possible as you may have postnatal depression and this often needs medical treatment. Postnatal depression is now a recognised condition and is a condition that develops without our control and can happen to anyone. Without treatment of some description negative feelings can worsen so it is important to try to get on top of it before this occurs.

Support groups

There are many support groups around for new parents, ranging from coffee mornings where you can have a general chat with other mums, to guided support groups that tackle specific issues such as breastfeeding, smoking, postnatal depression or counselling.

It is important to find out what is available in your area as you may be unaware of opportunities you would be interested in. Do not feel as though you would not fit in with the group because of your age, remember there are now more mothers in their 30s and beyond than before so the chances are there may be more parents nearer to your age than younger mums.

Please speak to your health visitor, library, local children's services department or nearest council office for more information on what is available to you.

Postnatal depression

Postnatal depression is now a highly recognised and serious issue. It is a term used to describe the depression that can happen after you have had a baby. It is not the baby blues that are experienced by many women and only last for a few days or weeks, it is in fact often a condition that goes unrecognised and untreated for several months gradually getting worse.

The euphoria of being pregnant and having a healthy baby is often what causes a lot of women not to seek help if they start feeling low. Some women feel guilty about being depressed or down, worry that people will think badly of them or even worry that the authorities will get involved and make changes in the family set-up.

All of these issues are very real to the woman, but are highly unlikely to happen if help is sought when it is first recognised. Those who do not seek help are more at risk of suffering further damage than those who admit they may have the condition and ask for help.

If at any time you feel as though you cannot cope, you can't sleep, eat or are irritable and struggling to look after either yourself or the baby, please speak to your midwife, health visitor, GP or other area of support immediately as help is out there and you will be surprised at how many women can relate to your story.

Being an older parent can bring its own struggles and challenges, and finding the energy to maintain a relationship, job and household as well as looking after your new baby carries a lot of pressure so it is no surprise that many women find they do need a bit of help from time to time. Do not feel guilty about this, after all, you are a human being not superwoman.

If you have suffered with depression at any stage in your life, please do tell your midwife during your booking appointment so that he or she knows you may be at risk of postnatal depression later on.

Managing with a baby

So, you've had the baby, have arrived home and are settling in to your new life. Congratulations, you have been on the most fantastic journey and now you and your family can learn to live together and have fun along the way!

It is easy to get swept away with the romance of having a new baby in the house and why not? You have waited long enough. But for some the reality comes crashing down soon after taking your little one home, proving why it is important to try to have some kind of plan in place as to how you are going to manage. Of course not all arrangements will go according to plan, but on the whole it may help to have a basic idea of how you will manage in the next few months.

Remember all the planning!

All the planning in the world is often not sufficient for the experience of having a new baby and all the intentions you had about how you were going to manage your time and raise your child may go flying out the window when you first meet your bundle of joy. To some degree, your baby's body clock and feeding regime will determine how you adapt, and, until you get home, find your feet and establish a routine, you will not be able to predict exactly how your life is going to change for the first few months of parenthood. Some parents are very lucky and are blessed with a baby who finds a good routine straightaway and sleeps well, eats well and is very content, while others will find they have a more demanding baby that needs attention more often. Do not worry too much if you need to feed your baby every few hours or they are difficult to settle as this will pass and you will become more expert in understanding their needs and learning their methods of communication. Believe it or not, within a few weeks many parents have learned what each type of cry means and can distinguish a hungry cry from the type of cry the baby gives when he or she simply wants a little cuddle or needs a nappy change.

Being mistaken for an older relative

Unfortunately, one of the hurdles an older parent has to face is the prospect of being mistaken for an older relative. Along with there being many older mothers these days, there are also many very young ones and often the public get so used to seeing young women with babies they forget that more and more women in their 40s and even some in their 50s are having children. Being mistaken for someone other than the child's mother can be very upsetting and far from a nice experience for those who it happens to. If this does happen to you, there are two ways of handling the situation; either you can simply ignore it and try to forget it happened, or you can be assertive and tell the person that you are in fact the very proud parent of your beautiful child.

Try not to let it worry you too much as your child is hardly likely to worry or even understand how old you are and won't be bothered by it at all; most children are very proud of their parents.

Keeping your energy levels up

Keeping your energy levels up can be difficult when you are busy looking after a newborn what with disturbed sleep, disrupted meal times and generally adjusting to the changes in your life but there are ways of making the most of your situation and finding ways of energising.

There are many opportunities open to new mothers and these include swimming classes or yoga sessions specifically introduced to new mothers, and many of them even allow you to take your baby along so you don't have to worry about childcare.

Remember, it is important to eat and drink well, especially if you are breastfeeding and this may mean that you eat little and often for a few months instead of having two or three larger meals during the day. Plenty of fresh fruit, dairy and vegetables will help keep your energy levels up, but if you're not keen on these types of food, why not blend them all together into a milkshake or smoothie? This way you will be getting all the health benefits and a nice tasting, cool drink too.

Finally, try to find time to treat yourself once a week with either a trip to the hair salon, getting a nice massage, going for a swim or to the gym (although not in the first few weeks after delivery) or even having a long bath with a good book. Ask your partner or a friend or relative to watch the baby for a few hours so you can spend time doing something that relaxes you as this will give you an energy boost later.

Summing Up

Caring for a new baby may come naturally to some people while others need to be shown the ropes.

Babies are well known for their demanding natures and this can last for several months (or even years) and coping with the pressure is not always easy.

By arming yourself with as much information as you can, and by spending time learning about your baby and letting him or her learn about you, are great ways of making the transition from pregnant woman to loving parent.

Give yourself time and don't let yourself feel pressured into being 'superwoman' as it can be very difficult adjusting to family life when you have only had yourself to look after for so long.

Good luck with your parenting and enjoy your baby!

'By arming yourself with as much information as you can, and by spending time learning about your baby and letting him or her learn about you, are great ways of making the transition from pregnant woman to loving parent.'

Need2Know

Help List

ARC (Antenatal Results and Choices)

73 Charlotte Street, London, W1T 4PN
Tel: 0207 631 0285 (helpline, Monday to Friday, 10am to 5.30pm)
info@arc-uk.org
www.arc-uk.org
An informative service offering parents the chance to gather all the necessary
information, helping them understand their choices regarding screening
procedures during pregnancy.

Askbaby.com

Fleet House, 8-12 New Bridge Street, London, EC4V 6AL
contact@askbaby.com
www.askbaby.com
Website giving information and advice on conception, pregnancy and
childbirth.

Association of Breastfeeding Mothers

PO Box 207, Bridgwater, Somerset, TA6 7YT
Tel: 08444 122 949 (helpline, Monday to Sunday, 9.30am to 10.30pm)
counselling@abm.me.uk
www.abm.me.uk
A charity founded by mothers for mothers to provide accurate information on
breastfeeding.

Babyandpregnancy.co.uk

www.babyandpregnancy.co.uk
Website including articles on all aspects of pregnancy and birth. You can
join and receive newsletters or even send in your own stories and share
experiences.

Babycentre

www.babycentre.co.uk

This website offers a comprehensive guide to the entire pregnancy, including detailed articles on the subject along with baby name suggestions, calculators and calendars. There is also a section for expectant fathers or partners and easy to use forums, blogs and photos.

Child Benefit Office

PO Box 1, Newcastle-upon-Tyne, NE88 1AA

Tel: 0845 302 1444 (helpline, Monday to Sunday, 8am to 8pm)

www.hmrc.gov.uk

A helpline set up to help you arrange your Child Benefit payments.

Department of Work and Pensions

Caxton House, Tothill Street, London, SW11 9DA

www.dwp.gov.uk

Government organisation dealing with all matters relating to employment. See the website for details of different departments and local office contact details.

Down's Syndrome Association

Langdon Down Centre, 2a Langdon Park, Teddington, TW11 9PS

Tel: 0845 230 0372 (helpline, Monday to Friday, 10am to 4pm)

info@downs-syndrome.org.uk

www.downs-syndrome.org.uk

A useful website that offers support, advice and reassurance for new parents of babies with Down's syndrome.

Family Planning Association (FPA)

50 Featherstone House, London, EC1Y 8QU

Tel: 0845 122 8690 (Monday to Friday, 9am to 6pm)

www.fpa.org.uk

The FPA is the UK's leading sexual health charity and aims to raise awareness of all aspects of sexual health, so informed choices can be made regarding all aspects of sex and family planning.

Fertility Expert

www.fertilityexpert.co.uk
This site offers a plethora of information on all aspects of fertility, offering advice on how to achieve pregnancy, getting help with fertility and the emotional issues surrounding the subject.

Infertility Network UK

Charter House, 43 St Leonards Road, Bexhill on Sea, East Sussex, TN40 1JA
Tel: 0800 008 7464
www.infertilitynetworkuk.com
The UK's leading infertility support network, offering information and advice guiding prospective parents through all aspects and issues of fertility and infertility.

Mothers Over 35

www.mothers35plus.co.uk
A useful website aimed at mothers over the age of 35, offering advice from women in similar situations with the opportunity to read the experiences of others, share your story, offer tips and ask questions. With sections aimed at fertility and increasing your chances of a natural conception, healthy pregnancy and problem-free delivery.

Mothers Over 40

www.mothersover40.com
Very similar to Mothers Over 35, only this website targets those 40 years and over.

National Childbirth Trust (NCT)

Alexandra House, Oldham Terrace, London, W3 6NH
Tel: 0300 330 0772 (pregnancy and birth line, Monday to Friday, 10am to 8pm)
0300 3300771 (breastfeeding line, Monday to Friday, 8am to 10pm)
0300 3300770 (enquiries line, Monday to Friday, 9am to 5pm)
www.nctpregnancyandbabycare.com

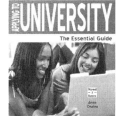
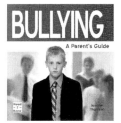